Perhaps the primary motivation for the study of psychology is simply the desire to understand behaviour. However, as Ann Searle reminds us in her introduction, if psychology is going to progress beyond 'common sense' argument, research must be conducted within a well-designed structure, results analysed and recorded carefully, and the findings presented clearly.

The aim of *Introducing research and data in psychology* is to help introductory-level students develop these abilities and, at the same time, to demonstrate that research design and data analysis are interesting and useful skills.

It introduces both experimental and non-experimental methods of research, and the analysis of data using both descriptive and inferential statistics. The uses, interpretation and calculation of common two-sample statistical tests are explained.

Ann Searle is a Principal Moderator for A-level and AS-level coursework.

Routledge Modular Psychology

Series editors: Cara Flanagan is the Assessor for the Associated Examining Board (AEB) and an experienced A-level author. Kevin Silber is Senior Lecturer in Psychology at Staffordshire University. Both are A-level examiners in the UK.

The *Routledge Modular Psychology* series is a completely new approach to introductory level psychology, tailor-made to the new modular style of teaching. Each short book covers a topic in more detail than any large textbook can, allowing teacher and student to select material exactly to suit any particular course or project.

The books have been written especially for those students new to higher-level study, whether at school, college or university. They include specially designed features to help with technique, such as a model essay at an average level with an examiner's comments to show how extra marks can be gained. The authors are all examiners and teachers at the introductory level.

The *Routledge Modular Psychology* texts are all user-friendly and accessible and include the following features:

- practice essays with specialist commentary to show how to achieve a higher grade
- chapter summaries to assist with revision
- progress and review exercises
- glossary of key terms
- summaries of key research
- further reading to stimulate ongoing study and research
- website addresses for additional information
- cross-referencing to other books in the series

ATYPICAL DEVELOPMENT AND ABNORMAL BEHAVIOUR

Psychopathology
John D. Stirling and Jonathan S.E. Hellewell

Therapeutic Approaches in Psychology
Susan Cave

BIO-PSYCHOLOGY

Cortical Functions
John Stirling (forthcoming)

The Physiological Basis of Behaviour: Neural and hormonal processes
Kevin Silber

States of Awareness
Evie Bentley (forthcoming)

COGNITIVE PSYCHOLOGY

Memory and Forgetting
John Henderson

Perception: Theory, development and organisation
Paul Rookes and Jane Willson (forthcoming)

COMPARATIVE PSYCHOLOGY

Reproductive Strategies
John Gammon (forthcoming)

DEVELOPMENTAL PSYCHOLOGY

Cognitive Development
David Cohen (forthcoming)

Early Socialisation: Sociability and attachment
Cara Flanagan (forthcoming)

PERSPECTIVES AND RESEARCH

Controversies in Psychology
Philip Banyard

Ethical Issues in Psychology
Mike Cardwell (forthcoming)

SOCIAL PSYCHOLOGY

Social Influences
Kevin Wren (forthcoming)

Interpersonal Relationships
Diana Dwyer (forthcoming)

STUDY GUIDE

Exam Success in AEB Psychology
Paul Humphreys

OTHER TITLES

Health Psychology
Anthony Curtis (forthcoming)

Sport Psychology
Matt Jarvis (forthcoming)

Introducing research and data in psychology
A guide to methods and analysis

Ann Searle

London and New York

First published 1999
by Routledge
11 New Fetter Lane, London EC4P 4EE

Simultaneously published in the USA and Canada
by Routledge
29 West 35th Street, New York, NY 10001

Typeset in Times by Routledge
Printed and bound in Great Britain by Clays Ltd, St Ives plc

British Library Cataloguing in Publication Data
A catalogue record for this book is available from the British Library

Library of Congress Cataloging in Publication Data
Searle, Ann
Introducing research and data in psychology/Ann Searle
Includes bibliographical references and index
1. Psychology–Research–Methodology. 2. Psychometrics.
I. Title.
BF76.5.S38 1999
150".7'2–dc21 98-33942

ISBN 0–415–18874–1 (hbk)
ISBN 0–415–18875–x (pbk)

Contents

Acknowledgements

The series editors and Routledge acknowledge the expert help of Paul Humphreys, Examiner and Reviser for A-level Psychology, in compiling the Study Aids section of each book in this series.

They also acknowledge the Associated Examining Board (AEB) for granting permission to use their examination material. The AEB do not accept responsibility for the answers or examiner comment in the Study Aids section of this book or any other book in the series.

Introduction

When you decided to study psychology you may well not have expected to have to study methodology and statistics. This may have been an unpleasant surprise to some of you and rather a shock to the system.

I am not going to attempt to justify here the emphasis that exam boards place on this area but rather to try to help you get over the shock. I well remember an experience in my own student career when a statistician came in and spoke what appeared to me to be complete gibberish for an hour. After a little gentle therapy, however, I actually came to quite enjoy the subject.

If you are thinking that psychology should be about understanding behaviour and experience you are quite correct. Don't ever forget this point. Some people do seem to get so wrapped up in measuring variables and number crunching that they seem to have lost touch with what presumably interested them in psychology in the first place – understanding behaviour. However, if psychology is going to progress beyond 'common sense' argument we must conduct well-designed research, record and analyse our results carefully, and present the findings in a form which is clear to everyone.

The aim of this book is to help you to do this, and also to show you that research design and data analysis are interesting and useful skills. Indeed, it can be argued that the ability to assess the quality of the research studies we may read or hear about via the media is a skill that all adults should possess.

A few practical points:

- Words highlighted in bold are included in the glossary at the back.
- Answers to the exercises are given in an appendix.
- Sample exam questions with marked examples of answers are included at the end of the text.

I hope you find the book useful.

Section One

Preliminaries

In everyday life we all speculate about the behaviour of others: what does your ex-girlfriend see in that wimp? why did your friend go to see that film *five* times? We want to understand our own behaviour as well: what did that dream of falling off the Eiffel Tower mean? why do you remember so much more information as soon as you leave the exam hall?

What is the difference between this everyday speculation and the practice of psychology? The main difference is that psychology tries to find answers by conducting systematic research in order to collect quantitative or qualitative data. Quantitative data involves measuring a variable using some numerical basis – for example, a bird-watcher counting how many birds visited their garden would be collecting quantitative data. Qualitative data, on the other hand, emphasises the interpretation and meaning attached to experiences – perhaps in this case a description of the enjoyment felt whilst watching those birds.

Psychology and common sense explanation

In everyday life our speculations are based on a limited range of observations from a limited range of people. Our own experiences are likely to be limited to a particular culture or subculture. Our speculations are often based on second-hand information, biased observations or subjective judgements. If psychology is to progress beyond the common sense level of explanation it must use better, more systematic methods.

As you study other areas of psychology you will see that not all psychological investigations fulfil these aims. (See Section Seven for further details.)

By learning about research methodology you will also be learning skills which will help you see the strengths, the flaws and the biases in other people's research.

Exercise 1

Would the following examples produce qualitative or quantitative data?

1 You count how many kittens there are in a litter.
2 You say, 'Ah – aren't they sweet'. Your friend says, 'Oh – I can't stand cats'.
3 You ask what my reaction was to a TV programme.
4 You count how many male and female characters have major roles in popular 'soaps'.

Academic psychology has attached great importance to the use of the **scientific method** – the dominant model of research used in the natural sciences (such as biology).

When using the scientific method it is the intention that research should be:

- based on **objective** observations or earlier research...
- from which are derived testable **hypotheses**...
- which are then evaluated via well-designed studies...
- which gather quantitative data...
- which is analysed and the results reported in such a way that others can examine, repeat or extend the findings.

Recently there has been increasing criticism of complete reliance on the quantitative-data-gathering aspects of the scientific method in psychology. Qualitative methods – such as the use of case studies – have always been a part of psychology, but were often seen as a supplement to 'real' research. Nowadays, especially in areas of psychology which deal with social issues, more use has been made of qualitative data by considering individuals' own experiences and their interpretations of situations – rather than merely measuring how they perform in those situations.

> Give four reasons why the observations that people make in everyday life about behaviour might be flawed.
>
> Exercise 2

It is assumed in this book that, whatever methods you choose to use, the order of events followed when conducting a piece of research would be:

- generating a research question;
- aims and hypotheses;
- designing your study; and

- analysing your results.

The book will also follow this order.

Choosing a research question, aims and hypotheses

You begin a piece of research with an idea that you wish to investigate. This may come from a teacher or a book, may be drawn from earlier research or from an observation of your own. It is important that you are clear in your own mind what the research question that you are intending to investigate actually is. If you begin with an initial broad area of interest you need to narrow this down to a specific area.

If the research is for coursework don't be too ambitious. It is easier to get a good mark if there is earlier research on which to base the study, and to write about in the introduction and the discussion section. It is also often easier if you have just one research question to investigate – you don't get twice the marks if you have two questions!

Having chosen your topic area, you will have to determine exactly what your aim is in the research. This means deciding two things:

- the *precise* area of the study;
- what the study is actually trying to achieve.

First in your report the *aim* should be stated reasonably precisely. 'The aim of this project is to look at gender differences' is too vague: what area of gender differences? what does 'look at' mean? Second you should explain the *purpose* of the study. Is it to extend or replicate someone else's work? to test a hypothesis based on a certain theory? to test an idea of your own? This has to be explained.

Hypotheses

> A hypothesis is a prediction or testable statement which a researcher aims to test to see if it is supported or rejected.

You will come across different types of hypotheses:

- the research hypothesis;
- the alternative hypothesis (also called the experimental hypothesis);
- the null hypothesis.

The **research hypothesis** is a general prediction made at the beginning of the study as to what you expect will happen. It is usually written at the end of the introduction. An example might be 'Short term memory declines with age'.

The **alternative** (or **experimental**) **hypothesis** is the *operational statement* of the research hypothesis. That means that it actually states the precise behaviours or responses that are going to be used to measure the variable under investigation. An example for the above research hypothesis might be 'Digit span for numbers in people over seventy years of age is shorter than digit span for numbers in people under twenty years of age'. The alternative or experimental hypothesis is what we hope we will find to be correct. It is a precise statement in terms of the measurements that will actually be made.

The **null hypothesis** is the hypothesis that a statistical test actually tests. Siegel (1956) calls it 'a hypothesis of no differences'. An example might be 'There is no difference in the digit span for numbers in people over seventy years of age and in people under twenty years of age'. In other words it is a statement that there is no difference (or **correlation**) between the scores you have collected on the variables you are measuring.

It seems to have become a convention in A-level psychology that the alternative/experimental and null hypotheses are written at the end of the introduction, but it can be argued that they should be written in the results section.

Which hypotheses are you expected to include when writing a report?

It is difficult to give a cut-and-dried answer to this question because conventions vary from institution to institution.

- It is usual to include a *research hypothesis* at the end of the introduction to the study. This states the prediction – which has been derived from the theory or previous research described in the introduction – that you are going to test.

- You may also be expected to **operationalise** the research hypothesis so that it is stated as an *alternative/experimental hypothesis*.
- It has become a convention in A-level reports that you also write out the *null hypothesis*. At university you may find you are asked why on earth you did this!

The practice that I am going to suggest here is that you certainly include a research hypothesis in the introduction, and that you write out an alternative and a null hypothesis if you are going to receive marks for them! Thus for A-level psychology I would advise you to include them; in Higher Education you should be guided by your lecturers. Where you include them is up to you: some people write them out at the end of the introduction, whereas some people write them out in the results section along with the statistics testing them.

> If you are taking an exam which involves short-answer questions on research methods and experimental design, you should know how to word all of these hypotheses as this is a common exam question.

Points on the wording of hypotheses

- You must be careful to word hypotheses clearly and precisely. While a *research hypothesis* might be phrased in fairly general terms, the *null* and *alternative/experimental hypotheses* must be 'operationalised'. 'Females are better with words than males' is far too vague: how will you measure how 'good' they are with 'words'? what age group are you testing? Your alternative/experimental hypothesis should indicate more precisely what you are going to test. Thus it might be 'Ten-year-old girls score more highly than ten-year-old boys in games of Scrabble'. You must make sure that the hypothesis clearly states *precisely* what you are investigating and identifies the variables that you are studying.
- There is some controversy over whether hypotheses should be written in the future tense ('There will be a difference…') or in the present tense ('There is a difference…'). Be guided by your lecturer

as to which they prefer. For a research hypothesis either is acceptable, but to be really correct alternative/experimental and null hypotheses should be written in the present tense.

- As the hypothesis is going to be tested in some way to see if it is supported or not, it is important that it only contains one **independent variable**. For example if your hypothesis stated 'There is a difference in the amount of aggression shown towards people who push into a queue if this person is a man or a woman or if they are over sixty or under twenty years old', what do you do if age seems to have an effect on aggression but gender doesn't? You cannot half accept a hypothesis. What you need is *two* hypotheses – one pertaining to gender and the other pertaining to age.

- Should you include the word *significant*? There is some debate as to whether 'significant' should be included in the hypothesis. Some teachers will expect you to write 'Drivers of family cars will be *significantly* more likely to stop at zebra crossings than drivers of sports cars'. Other teachers will not expect you to include it. This is a controversial issue rather beyond the scope of this book. Exam boards will accept either version, but most modern statistics books do not include the word 'significant'.

Some further examples

If you were conducting research into whether there is a relationship between grades in exams taken at the ages of sixteen and eighteen, your *research hypothesis* might be that 'Students who do well in exams at sixteen will also do well in exams when they are eighteen'. Your *alternative hypothesis* might be 'There is a correlation between the grades students obtain in exams at the age of sixteen and the grades they obtain at the age of eighteen,' while the *null hypothesis* might be 'There is no correlation between grades obtained at the age of sixteen and grades obtained at the age of eighteen'.

If you were researching helping behaviour your *research hypothesis* might be that 'People in rural areas are more likely to help someone than people in large cities'. Your *alternative hypothesis* might be 'A young woman who drops her shopping outside a village shop will receive help more quickly than a young woman who drops her shopping outside a large city superstore'. Your null hypothesis might be that 'There will be no difference in how quickly a young woman receives help who drops her shopping outside a village shop or a large city superstore'.

Exercise 3

Write a suitable alternative hypothesis and a suitable null hypothesis for a study with the research hypothesis that 'Too many cooks spoil the broth'.

Why do we have all these types of hypotheses?

Having collected your data you will probably carry out a statistical test which tells you the **probability** that your results are due to chance. As explained above, the statistical test is testing the *null hypothesis* – testing whether the **samples** of scores that you have collected are drawn from the same **population** of scores.

We use statistics to indicate the level of probability of obtaining a particular result. If the probability that the scores we have collected are all drawn from the same population of scores is very low (usually 5 per cent or less) we may choose to accept the alternative/experimental hypothesis. (See later section on probability, pp. 184–90, for more details.)

Remember   The *research hypothesis* states the general prediction that we are going to test in our study.

The *alternative* or *experimental hypothesis* operationalises this prediction in precise terms.

The *null hypothesis* states that there is no difference or no correlation in the scores of the populations that we are testing.

Directional and non-directional hypotheses

If the hypothesis predicts the expected direction of the result then it is called a **directional** (or **one-tailed**) **hypothesis**. For example:

'School children who eat breakfast do *better* at school than those who do not', or
'There is a *positive* correlation between height and weight'.

If the hypothesis just says that there will be a difference or a correlation – but does not predict the direction – then it is called a **non-directional** (or **two-tailed**) **hypothesis**. For example:

'Dogs and cats differ in how quickly they learn a maze' (note that the hypothesis doesn't state which will learn fastest), or
'There is a correlation between exam results and hours spent watching TV' (note that it doesn't say if watching a lot of TV will be related to better or worse exam results).

When do you choose a directional hypothesis?

Traditionally you might select a directional hypothesis when the weight of earlier research makes it possible to make a clear prediction. For example if there have been five or six studies that have found dogs *do* learn mazes faster than cats then you might feel able to say 'Dogs learn a simple maze faster than cats'. *If you do select a directional hypothesis you should justify this choice in your report.*

There are some controversies associated with this, however. MacRae (1994) argues that in psychology we can never really make sufficiently clear predictions to justify the use of directional hypotheses. It is also argued by some statisticians that you should not choose a directional hypothesis if you are collecting data at a nominal level. Nominal categories are, by definition, unordered and so it is not logical to select a directional hypothesis. (There is further discussion of this point in Section Twelve, pp. 153–7, when discussing the chi-square test.)

If you do select a directional hypothesis, you can't have it both ways! If your data comes out the opposite way to your prediction you *must* accept the null hypothesis – you must *not* accept the research hypothesis, even if the data shows a big difference in the 'wrong' direction. So if you predict dogs will learn your maze faster than cats, and then you find the cats are fastest (as they probably would be given the contrary nature of cats), you can't change your mind and say 'Oh great – I've got a significant result anyway'. You haven't got a significant result. You've got a non-significant result because your particular prediction has not been supported by the evidence. (This is why MacRae suggests that directional hypotheses should not be used.)

Exercise 4

It is a common exam question to ask candidates to write a suitable hypothesis for a study, so make sure you practise this. (In an exam you can often use words from the exam paper to produce a clear, precise hypothesis.)

1   For each of the following studies write a suitable directional alternative/experimental hypothesis, a suitable non-directional alternative/experimental hypothesis and a null hypothesis:

   (a) A psychologist conducts a study on students to see if the amount of fish eaten affects IQ scores.
   (b) A study investigates the length of time babies spend looking at simple shapes or human faces.
   (c) A gardener compares the number of tomatoes produced by plants in 'grow bags' or in the ground.
   (d) A psychologist investigates the relationship between IQ at the age of eleven and IQ at the age of sixteen.
   (e) A bus company investigates the relationship between the fares charged over a five-year period and the number of passengers catching their buses.

2   Identify whether these hypotheses are directional or non-directional:

   (a) Young children prefer chocolate to cabbage.
   (b) Lack of sleep makes people irritable.
   (c) Girls talk more than boys.
   (d) The quality of service in a café affects its popularity.
   (e) Age affects short-term memory.

The hypotheses above are not well-phrased. They are not operationalised because they don't explain how the variables involved will be measured. They need rephrasing to make them more precise. As a further exercise you could consider how the variables involved could be operationalised.

Independent and dependent variables

It was stated earlier that when you write your research hypothesis it must be operationalised and that this means that you need to identify the **variables** that you are going to study.

- The word 'variable' is used to describe something that alters when we are conducting research.

In experimental research a variable is deliberately altered by the researcher so that the effects on another variable can be measured.

- A variable which is manipulated in research is called an independent variable or an IV.
- A variable which is measured is called a **dependent variable** or a DV.

Learn the jargon now.

Can you think of a mnemonic to help you remember it? or will you have to repeat it over and over again until you are sure you know it? It is important you get this right!

You alter an IV; you measure a DV.

Not all variables can be controlled by the researcher. Such uncontrolled variables can alter in an unsystematic way. (The issue of uncontrolled variables is dealt with in Section Seven.)

When using the *experimental method* we alter an independent variable and see if this produces a change in a dependent variable. If it does, and we cannot see any uncontrolled factors in the situation that might have affected the result, we assume that the change in the IV has led to the change we observed in the DV. In other words we infer that there is a causal relationship between the two variables.

Exercise 5

Identify the independent variables and dependent variables in the following experiments:

1 One group of students is kept awake for forty-eight hours and their ability to remember a list of twelve words is compared with that of a group who have slept normally.

2 The reaction time of fifteen people who have just run a mile is compared with that of a group who have just driven cars for a mile.

3 A researcher presents sparrows with different-sized bugs. Some are smaller than their usual food, some are the same size, some are larger but still edible. The type of bugs eaten by the sparrows is noted.

4 Participants are given the description of a person to read. All descriptions are identical except that some participants are told the person is of the same ethnic group as themselves, while others are told they are from a different group. Having read the description participants are asked to select characteristics they think describe the person.

5 An occupational psychologist measures the number of packets of cereal that are packed in thirty minutes if workers are alone, in a group of six or in a group of twelve.

Section Two

Preliminaries

Having decided upon your research question and your hypotheses the next thing that you will have to decide before you begin your research is exactly what *method* you will use. Methods fall into three groups:

- *experimental methods*: laboratory or field experiments.
- *natural experiments and quasi-experiments*.

- *non-experimental methods*: such as investigations using correlation, observation, questionnaires and surveys, interviews, psychological tests, **content analysis** and **discourse analysis**.

The use of the *experimental method* has dominated psychology in the twentieth century, with emphasis placed on **quantitative data**. Recently, however, there has been criticism of over-reliance on such methods and a growth of interest in *non-experimental approaches* and also on **qualitative research** and analysis. In fact, it is often the case that good research has used a variety of methods for both data collection and for analysis. Even in a strictly controlled laboratory experiment much can be learned from talking to the participants about what they thought was happening and why they behaved as they did.

For these reasons some exam syllabuses may ask you to use both qualitative and quantitative methods of analysis in your own coursework.

Research methods are sometimes divided into experimental and non-experimental methods but, in fact, there is no clear dividing line between the two, and there is some controversy over which label best fits *natural* and *quasi-experiments*.

The experimental method

There are two main defining features of the experimental method:

- The researcher alters one element or variable (called the *independent variable*) and looks to see if there is an effect on another variable (called the *dependent variable*). (These terms are explained in Section One on p. 13.)
- It must be possible to randomly allocate participants to the different conditions for the research to be a true experiment. If it is not possible for you to select twenty people, put all the names in a hat, draw out ten of them to put in Group A and then the other ten to put in Group B, then it is not a true experiment but a quasi-experiment.

For example if you were investigating the effect of noise on memory and wanted two groups of participants – one group who are asked to learn a list of words in noisy conditions and a second group who are asked to learn the same list in quiet conditions – it would be possible to select thirty people and put *any one of them in either group* (i.e. it would be possible to randomly allocate any participant to either group). However, if you were investigating whether men or women have better memories it would be impossible to do this – the men would be in one group and the women in the other and you could not alter this! Thus such research is not regarded as a true experiment but as a quasi-experiment. (See p. 21 for more information on quasi-experiments.)

True experiments can be divided into two types:

* laboratory experiments
* field experiments

Laboratory experiments

Here the research is conducted in a setting where the researcher can control as many variables as possible. This is not always an actual laboratory. It should be possible to change the independent variable (e.g. noise level) and keep all other variables the same. This is achieved most easily by bringing the participants into a laboratory setting. In Asch's research into conformity (1955) all the participants were tested in the same room under the same conditions so he could ensure that, for example, what people saw, where they sat, what others said, etc., was the same for each participant. Compare this to attempting to do research into conformity in a normal classroom setting.

Advantages of laboratory experiments

* They allow for the precise control of variables.
* It is far easier to replicate this type of research, so other researchers can see if they obtain the same results.
* They allow cause-and-effect relationships to be established.
* It is possible, within ethical constraints, to engineer situations which rarely occur and observe reactions to these situations under controlled conditions. For example the effect of questioning on the memories of eyewitnesses can be studied under laboratory conditions.

- It is possible to use technical apparatus – which cannot be used in more natural settings – to take accurate measurements (e.g. of stress reactions).

Our ultimate aim is often to find out which variables are responsible for *causing* the events that we observe. We see a world which keeps changing and we want to know *what factors are causing these changes*.

It is only by using the *experimental method* that we can play around with one variable and see what effect this has on something else. If we alter one variable (perhaps the length of delay between learning a list of words and recalling it) and we find a change in what we are measuring (how many words people remember) then we assume that there is a causal relationship between the two things. This is the logic of experimental design, and it is only by conducting experiments that we can make such causal assumptions.

Disadvantages of laboratory experiments

- The behaviour that can be studied in a laboratory is limited in its range. There are many behaviours which cannot be studied in such an artificial situation with any validity (e.g. interpersonal attraction).
- The high level of control may make the situation very artificial (e.g. memory experiments have often involved learning lists of nonsense syllables such as FEP, JUV, BEX, etc.). How often do people do this in real life?
- It may be difficult to **generalise** from laboratory experiments to other settings. (To put this into jargon, laboratory experiments can lack **ecological validity**.)
- People may behave differently in a laboratory to the way in which they would behave in their normal day-to-day lives. This problem is referred to as **demand characteristics** – the participants will try to guess what the study is about and what they decide will affect their behaviour. Laboratories can be intimidating to people not used to such an environment and they may not behave naturally.

Field experiments

In a field experiment the same methods of manipulating the independent variable and measuring the dependent variable are used but they are applied in the participants' natural environment. An example would be Piliavin *et al.*'s (1969) work on helping behaviour when an actor collapsed on the New York subway pretending to be, for example, drunk or blind. The Piliavins could manipulate variables (such as the actor pretending to be blind or drunk) and measure how long it took for help to be given, but this was all done in a natural setting.

You might consider the *ethics* of conducting such research in natural settings. What ethical issues arise?

Advantages of field experiments

- It is possible to study cause-and-effect relationships as one variable is manipulated and the effects on another are measured.
- Field experiments have much higher *ecological validity* as they are conducted in a natural setting and so it is perhaps more likely that the findings can be generalised to other settings.
- Participants may not know that their behaviour is being studied so they are not affected by *demand characteristics*.

Disadvantages of field experiments

- It is not possible to control extraneous variables so precisely as in a laboratory.
- They may be more expensive and time-consuming than laboratory work.
- Ethical issues may arise if it is not possible to have the **informed consent** of those taking part or to **debrief** people later.
- It may be difficult to replicate the studies precisely.

Exercise 6

Make a list of two laboratory experiments and two field experiments that you have met in different areas of psychology.

Compare them on the following issues:

1 Was there precise control of variables? Were some variables which could affect the results uncontrolled?
2 Would it be easy to replicate the study?
3 Could the findings be generalised to other settings (i.e. do the studies have ecological validity)?
4 Are there ethical problems, such as lack of informed consent or debriefing?
5 How might demand characteristics affect the behaviour of the participants?

Natural experiments and quasi-experiments

Natural experiments

In a **natural experiment** a variable changes and the effects on another variable can be measured but:

- the changes are not actually manipulated by the researcher, and
- there is no control over the allocation of the participants to the different conditions.

Example

If a school introduced a new reading scheme for one class the effect of this variable on reading skills could be investigated by comparing this class with a class being taught on the old reading scheme. There would be a naturally occurring **experimental group** for whom something had changed and a naturally occurring **control group** for whom the status quo is maintained. Such research would not be a true experiment because the research cannot actually decide which child will be in which group and the manipulation of the independent variable (which reading scheme was used) was not under the control of the researcher.

Advantages of natural experiments

- The situation is a natural one and any change would occur anyway so there is high ecological validity.
- The effect on one variable resulting from a change in another can be observed as long as other variables which could affect the result can be controlled. Thus cause-and-effect relationships may be inferred – although care must be taken because of the possibility of **confounding variables**.

Disadvantages of natural experiments

- There may be many uncontrolled variables making it impossible to isolate the effect of a particular independent variable.
- The fact that the groups may know they are being studied by the researcher may affect their behaviour (the problem of demand characteristics).
- Natural situations for studying certain variables may arise very rarely and so not be available for study at the time of the research.
- Ethical considerations can arise because there may be problems of obtaining the informed consent of participants or because a new treatment which may be advantageous is given to one group but not to another.

Quasi-experiments

In a **quasi-experiment** the allocation of participants to the different conditions *cannot actually be manipulated* by the researcher. Experimental procedures are used but *random allocation of the participants to the conditions is not possible*.

Example

If you are comparing the drawing ability of three- and six-year-olds, a child is either aged three and is in one group or is aged six and is in the other group. You can apply other controls and the effect of the variable 'age' on another variable 'drawing skill' can be studied, but it is obviously impossible to *randomly allocate* children to one or other of the groups: they are either three or six years old.

In a quasi-experiment the independent variable is something the researcher cannot actually alter – such as whether people smoke or not, the type of therapy that has been given to people with a certain disorder, and so on. An independent variable can be identified and its effects on a dependent variable can be studied, but random allocation of participants to the experimental groups is impossible.

If it were possible for the researcher to randomly assign some people to a therapy and some to a control group, then this would be a true experiment.

Advantages of quasi-experiments

- With many variables this is the only possible type of experiment that can be done.
- If it is possible to control extraneous variables it is possible to infer cause-and-effect relationships.

Disadvantages of quasi-experiments

- There may be other differences between the two groups that cannot be controlled, making it impossible to infer cause-and-effect relationships. For example when comparing three- and six-year-olds one group will not have started school and the other will have done.

Whether or not natural and quasi-experiments are regarded as experiments depends upon the strictness of the definition used – and this is a controversial area. Because there is some debate over this issue, if you are required to carry out research which is either experimental or non-experimental it *may* be possible to argue a case for natural and quasi-experiments fitting into either group. For example the AEB has issued a statement as follows (note the last phrase!):

It is, in practice, very difficult to identify the precise boundaries between 'experimental' and 'non-experimental' research…a natural experiment might therefore be correctly regarded as either experimental or non-experimental, depending on the strictness of definition with which the term is defined. The

Board will accept such work as either experimental or non-experimental *if the candidate makes an appropriate case for it.*
(AEB, December 1996; my italics)

You should realise, however, that, as a student, the purpose of conducting your own research is to give you a deeper understanding of the different methods available to you. It is therefore a mistake to limit your experience to the use of similar – if not identical – methods if you have a wider choice.

Are the following natural experiments or quasi-experiments? Explain why you have come to your decision in each case.

1 A researcher compares the detail in drawings of faces by four- and eight-year-olds.
2 Weight-gain in premature babies is measured before and after a hospital introduces the use of sheepskin in babies' incubators.
3 A gardener compares the growth of his tomato plants with that of plants he gave to his sister who lives twenty miles away.
4 The amount of time it takes male and female eighteen-year-olds to get ready for a night out is compared.

Exercise 7

Introduction to non-experimental methods

In many cases it may be more appropriate to study behaviour using alternative methods to the experiment: for instance *observational methods* may be used when the researcher wishes to obtain evidence about behaviour in a real-life setting. It is often good practice to use non-experimental methods alongside experimental, so that data is collected in a variety of ways.

The following non-experimental methods are dealt with here: observations, content analysis, **case studies**, interviews and correlations.

You may be required to complete only a certain number of course-work studies to fulfil the requirements of your course, *but* you will find your understanding of research methods is increased if you carry out some quick investigations using a variety of methods which you do not necessarily fully write up.

Observational methods

Confusion sometimes arises between observation as a *technique* to gather data (which can be used in a range of research methods) and the *observational method*. For instance in Bandura's famous 'Bobo'-doll experiments (1963), he *observed* the behaviour of children playing with 'Bobo'. This is an example of the observational technique: Bandura's research used the *experimental method* (comparing the behaviour of children who had seen a film of an adult abusing 'Bobo' with a control group who had not), but he used observational techniques to collect his data.

With the observational method, as used by Schaffer and Emerson in their study of attachment in Scottish babies (1964), there is no such manipulation of a variable by the researcher. The babies were observed at home at four-week intervals as normal family life continued. In such a study the researcher observes *the freely chosen behaviour of a person or animal* and observes a *naturally occurring behaviour which is not manipulated in any way.*

Studies using the observational method can be of different types:

- *naturalistic observation*: observing behaviour in its natural setting.
- *participant observation*: when the observer joins the group being studied.
- *controlled observation*: when the researcher has some measure of control over the environment.

For all of these studies, the observations may vary in the extent to which they are *structured or unstructured* and the *participants may or may not know that they are being observed.*

Besides being used as the sole technique in research projects observational studies may also be used as initial pilot studies to collect data before devising experiments. (For example, Piaget observed his own children then derived hypotheses from this work which were explored experimentally by himself and others).

1 Think of another experiment you have studied which uses the observational technique and another study using the observational method, and explain why these examples are appropriate.
2 Are the following observational studies or studies using observational techniques? If they are observational studies, what type of study are they?

   (a) A student observes how often parents talk to their children in a supermarket.
   (b) A trainee teacher joins various classes as a student to observe different lecturing styles.
   (c) The speed at which woodlice run away from red or blue light is measured.
   (d) The types of play shown by three-year-old children in a specially prepared nursery are observed.
   (e) The behaviour of people on a train is compared when a woman appears to faint or a man appears to faint.

Points to consider when planning observational studies

When conducting an observational study it is important to be watchful of **observer bias** and prejudice. It is all too easy to see what you expect to see.

This can be guarded against by:

- training observers,
- having a structured checklist for recording the observation,
- having at least two observers and comparing their results (this is referred to as checking **inter-judge** or **inter-observer reliability**).

If the observers are aware of the hypothesis it is very easy for them to record what they expect to see rather than what actually occurs. As a control researchers may choose to use observers who do not know the nature of the hypothesis being tested or the aim of the research.

When conducting an observational study you must be clear *exactly* what it is that you are going to observe and you must *operationalise* the variables involved i.e. you must *define precisely what it is that will be recorded*. It is no use saying you will observe 'aggression in children'. How are you defining aggression? Will you include shouting? or only physical contact? How will you decide if a push is an accident or deliberate? In other words you must define the 'operations' which constitute your definition of aggression by devising a careful list of the precise behaviours for which you will be looking.

Exercise 9

How might you 'operationalise':

1 the aggression shown by four-year-olds at a birthday party?
2 the aggression shown by your cat?

The next step will be to do a **pilot study** to see if your proposed methods of measuring the variable you are interested in actually works in practice. You should also check the *inter-judge reliability* in your study. If two observers record the same event using your checklist, do they agree as to the categories of behaviour that they have seen?

As with other non-experimental designs, it is not possible to draw conclusions about cause and effect from observational studies as there is no manipulation of any variable by the researcher.

Naturalistic observation

Here spontaneous behaviour is recorded in a natural setting. Examples you may meet are Brown's study of language development (1973), the Robertsons' study of children in hospital (1971) and Goodall's studies of the Gombe chimps (1978). The observer does not interfere with or manipulate the behaviour being observed.

The observations would generally be *non-participant* (the observer tries to be unobtrusive so that the participants are unaware of being observed) but this can prove difficult. You may have seen on television the famous clip of David Attenborough and the gorillas – the gorillas seemed determined he would participate! Nowadays researchers may well record events using video cameras with the tapes being analysed later.

Advantages of naturalistic observation

- Such studies have high ecological validity: it can be argued that behaviour only occurs in its true form in natural settings.
- Material can be collected about naturally occurring situations which it would be unethical to deliberately engineer (e.g. children's behaviour when separated from their carers).
- Naturalistic observations are very useful research tools when investigating a new area. They enable hypotheses to be generated which can then be studied experimentally.

Disadvantages of naturalistic observation

- It is difficult to control confounding variables (other things which alter that could affect the results).
- If people or animals realise that they are being watched they may not behave naturally.
- It is difficult to replicate naturalistic observation studies so it may be hard to check the reliability and validity of the findings.
- It is difficult to be an objective observer. To control for this it is usual to have at least two observers and to check for **inter-rater reliability**. It is easier to do this if material has been recorded.
- It is not possible to draw conclusions about cause and effect because there is no manipulation of an independent variable.

27

• Ethical issues may arise:

   (a) With *humans*: the British Psychological Society guidelines state that people should only be observed without their consent in situations where they might expect to be observed by strangers.
   (b) With *non-human animals*: when studying non-human animals observers must be careful not to disturb them in any way.

Participant observation

In participant observation the researcher is to some extent part of the group of individuals being observed. The researcher takes an active part in the situation being studied e.g. Rosenhan's famous 'schizophrenia' study (1973) when eight people pretended to hear voices to gain admittance to mental hospitals as patients, and then observed the behaviour of the staff; Marsh, Rosser and Harre's study of the behaviour of football fans (1978).

The extent of the participation can vary:

1   a full participant hides their role of observer and pretends to be a group member;
2   a participant as observer does not hide their research interest but joins in fully with the group;
3   an observer as participant has the observer role uppermost and is accepted into the group only as an observer.

It is possible to argue that in most *of psychological research the researcher is a participant observer. For example in most experiments the researcher is not only recording the response of the participant but is also* part *of the experimental situation. (See Section Five, 'The experiment as a social situation'.)*

Advantages of participant observation

• Participation in the group may increase the observer's understanding and add to the richness of the data collected. This is

especially true if they become a long-term member of the group and the group grows to trust them.
- There may be access to data which is unobtainable by other methods.
- Ecological validity is higher than in laboratory studies.

- The fact that the researcher joins the group may alter the group in some way.
- In full participant observation the researcher has to rely on memory – they cannot make notes as they go.
- It is easy to become emotionally involved with the group and then it becomes hard to remain an objective observer.
- The study may not be replicable so the reliability and validity of the data cannot be checked.
- It may be difficult to generalise from the results.
- Ethical issues may arise if the participants have not given their consent to the study.

Controlled observations

Here, spontaneous behaviour is observed, but in a situation which, to some extent, has been manipulated and controlled by the researcher. Probably the most widely quoted example is the study on attachment behaviour in a strange situation by Ainsworth, Bell and Stayton (1971), where mothers and babies were observed in a specially prepared room and various events were arranged (stranger enters, mother leaves, etc.). It is actually very difficult to decide if this research is a controlled observation or an experiment using observational techniques!

Advantages of controlled observations

- This method has much in common with naturalistic observation – especially if the participants are young children or non-human animals who will not be suspicious of the manipulation of the environment.

- As the researcher has some control of the environment it is possible to control some confounding variables.
- It may be easy to record the behaviour on VCR for later analysis.

Disadvantages of controlled observations

- If the setting is unfamiliar to the participants the behaviour may not be completely natural.
- Participants are likely to know they are being observed which may affect their behaviour.
- It is unlikely to be possible to study cause-and-effect relationships.

Exercise 10

1 Name two controls that you would wish to include if you were conducting a study in which you observed whether a football team played more skilfully at home or away.
2 What is meant by the following terms:

   inter-judge reliability,
   participant observation, and
   operationalising variables?

Recording and interpreting data from observational studies

Data may be recorded in a variety of ways:

- making notes on the spot;
- filling in checklists on the spot;
- recording observations by speaking into a tape recorder on the spot;
- making a video or film recording and using any of the above methods at a later date.

If it is not possible to record the scene for later analysis various methods can be used.

- In **time interval sampling** an individual is observed for several short periods – such as thirty seconds – in a longer session such as an hour – and the presence or absence of a certain behaviour is noted for each period.
- In **event sampling** a record is made every time a certain event occurs.
- In **time point sampling** the observer records the behaviour of an individual at fixed points in time, for example, every five minutes.

It is possible to collect both *qualitative* and *quantitative data* in an observation.

Observers may use *rating systems* in which the quality or intensity of a particular behaviour is assessed, and these may involve the **subjective** interpretation of feelings. They could also use objective *coding systems* in which, for example, the number of times a particular event occurs in a particular time period is ticked. In Ainsworth, Bell and Stayton's study of attachment patterns of infants in a strange situation (1971) the amount of eye contact between infant and mother was noted (quantitative data) but also the sensitivity shown by mothers was assessed (qualitative data).

Depending on the nature of the enquiry recordings can be highly *structured* or *unstructured*. An observational study testing a specific hypothesis would be likely to be more structured than an exploratory pilot study.

1   In an observational study of aggressive behaviour in eight-year-olds conducted in a school playground, explain how the following methods could be used to collect quantitative data:

   time interval sampling; event sampling; time point sampling

2   Explain why inter-judge reliability could be a problem, and how this could be checked.

3   Describe one type of qualitative data that could be collected.

Exercise 11

Content analysis

Content analysis has many similarities with the observational method but what is studied is not direct behaviour but a representation of behaviour in a film, a book, a speech, and so on. For example it could be used to study the gender stereotypes current in a culture by analysing popular films made by members of that culture. *Content analysis is a systematic and objective method of providing a quantitative description of any such communication.*

There are two parts to the process:

- an interpretational aspect which involves deciding which categories are meaningful in terms of what you are investigating. Will you count the number of male and female characters in a film? sort them into 'active' or 'passive'? old or young? what they look like? how much they say? What is relevant to what *you* want to study?
- a mechanical aspect which involves organising and subdividing the material using the criteria you have decided to use.

For example if you were doing a content analysis of children's books you would first decide exactly *why* you were doing this study and exactly *what* you were going to analyse. If you were interested in the development of reading skills you might analyse word length, mean number of words per sentence, and so on. However, if you were interested in gender bias then the number of characters of each gender, their activities and their roles would be more relevant.

You will see that a content analysis – like any observational study – requires very careful planning if it is to be successful.

A brief summary of the steps to be followed is as follows:

- Narrow down and clarify your *aim*. What *exactly* are you studying?
- Do you have a *research hypothesis* based on, for example, a theory, an observation or previous research? or is your study more in the nature of a pilot study where it may be inappropriate to have a specific hypothesis?
- Decide on the materials to be studied. This will involve *sampling* – if you are interested in gender bias in adverts you won't study every

single advert so must decide how you will select the sample that will be analysed.

- Decide exactly which variables you are going to measure.
- Devise a checklist or coding system to measure these variables. When you do this you should also think about how you are going to analyse the information you collect.
- Do a pilot study to see if your coding system works.
- Collect your data.
- Summarise and analyse your results so that your findings are presented in a clear and concise fashion.

Example

An example of a content analysis is the work of Graebner (1972) on sexism in children's reading books of the 1960s. She collected information from popular children's books on the sex of all the children shown in pictures, the main characters, the passive characters, the active characters, the dependent or independent characters and the character taking part in 'boy' or 'girl' activities.

The results are predictable – and encouraging only if you believe that a woman's place is at the kitchen sink. You certainly wouldn't find many men there in these books – unless plumbing work is needed!

Try to conduct a small observational study or content analysis so that you have first hand experience of the difficulties. Observational research sounds a lot easier than it actually is!

Case studies

A case study involves the use of non-experimental methods to conduct an in-depth study of an individual or small group. Detailed descriptions of behaviour, detailed interviews, etc. are conducted and interpreted, plus it is usual to gather a *case history* (a history of relevant aspects of the person's life so far).

33

Information may be gathered from both *primary sources* (such as direct observation or interviews) or from *secondary sources* (such as school and medical records or friends and relatives).

Case studies are very different to many other approaches used by psychologists. They are an example of an **idiographic approach** (concerned with the individual) rather than the more common **nomothetic approach** (establishing general patterns of behaviour) followed by most researchers. They often use *qualitative methods* of analysis (stressing the *interpretation* of material) rather than the more common *quantitative methods* used elsewhere (which collect *numerical* data).

> Do not confuse case studies with single participant experiments which involve manipulation of variables by the researcher.

Advantages of case studies

- They offer a rich, in-depth insight into the individual or group, being far more detailed than most research and recognising the uniqueness of each individual. This is their particular strength.
- They acknowledge the importance of the *subjective* feelings of those studied.
- Sometimes case studies can highlight extraordinary behaviour and open up new areas of study which could not possibly be engineered in any other way because of ethical considerations. For example work on children suffering extreme deprivation in their early years.
- Sometimes the findings of a case study can contradict the predictions of a well-established theory (e.g. Skeels' work on deprived babies showed that intelligence scores are not fixed at birth but can be affected by life experiences – see Skeels 1966).
- Case studies into similar phenomena can be pooled to create a mass of detailed information which can be sorted and analysed and may reveal unexpected variables which can then be investigated further.

- Case studies are valuable exploratory tools which can lead to the generation of hypotheses for further research.

Disadvantages of case studies

- Case studies cannot be replicated so it is not possible to check the **reliability** of the results (i.e. whether or not the same results would be obtained if the study was repeated).
- It is not possible to generalise from the results obtained in the case study of one person to the rest of the population. The individual being studied may be atypical.
- The researcher's own *subjective feelings* may influence the data collection. It can be difficult for the researcher to remain objective if the work requires a great deal of contact with the person being studied.
- The researcher may be *selective* about what appears in the final report. It is indeed very unlikely that all the data collected will be reported (e.g. in the case of Gardner and Gardner's study [1969] in which they investigated whether a chimp, Washoe, could learn sign language, only selected material from an enormous quantity of filmed data was released when the first reports were published).
- If a case study includes **retrospective** material (i.e. material is collected about events that occurred some time earlier and which was not recorded at the time) this may be inaccurate; for example, in a case study of an adult it can be difficult to ascertain if recollections of early childhood events are accurate.

Explain how each of the words or phrases below could be used to comment on the case study method:

idiographic, qualitative, highly detailed, recognise the subjective feelings of the participant, ethical issues, reliability, challenge to accepted theory, retrospective data, generalisability, subjective, selective interpretation by researcher.

Exercise 12

Conducting a case study

Conducting a case study is not an easy option. As with any research you need to have a clear *aim* before you begin the study. The methods that are used can be varied depending upon the age of the subject of the study, the purpose for which it is being conducted, and so on. They may include interviews, observations, the study of records on that person and the use of psychometric tests, among other approaches.

There are also complex ethical issues to consider – *especially if your sole reason for conducting this study is for exam coursework*. Is it justifiable to use material related to mental health or antisocial behaviour in this way? Are students qualified to conduct case studies involving sensitive issues? Probably not.

Interviews

Interview methods vary according to the extent to which they are *structured*:

- In an **unstructured** (or **non-directive**) **interview** the person answering the questions (the interviewee) can talk about anything they like. In this kind of interview much *qualitative data* is likely to be collected about *how* the person talks, when pauses occur in the conversation, etc. as well as *what* is said.
- In a **semi-structured** (or **informal**) **interview** (also sometimes called a **clinical interview**) there is an overall aim as to what data should be collected but the questions asked can vary widely from person to person. The next question to be asked is determined by the response to the previous question. Again *qualitative data* may be collected. Such a technique was used by Jean Piaget in his work on children's intellectual and moral development. If there is a little more structure it might be called a *guided interview*. This is where the interviewer has a directive as to the topics to be covered but it is left to them how to order and phrase the questions.
- In a **structured** (or **formal**) **interview** there are preset questions to be asked in the same order to each person. Questions may be open-ended, that is many answers are possible (e.g. 'Why do you enjoy listening to music?'), or have closed answers, that is a fixed choice

of answers is offered. (e.g. 'What type of music do you enjoy? Rock/Pop/Jazz/Classical' or 'Do you listen to music? Yes/No')

The case study method could well include the use of interviews.

Advantages with unstructured interviews

- They are a rich source of data – especially qualitative data – relating to what interviewees themselves feel is important.
- The interviewees should feel relaxed and so answer fully.

Disadvantages with unstructured interviews

- Different data will be collected from each person so comparisons are difficult.
- Analysis may be difficult.
- *Reliability* is low as the interview cannot be repeated.
- *Inter-judge reliability* may be low as different people may disagree over interpretation.
- As with all interviews, there may be a tendency for the interviewee to say what they think the interviewer wants to hear.

Advantages with semi-structured interviews

- The interviewer can be flexible and follow the line of thinking of each interviewee.
- The interviewee is likely to feel relaxed.
- Data will have been collected on the same general topics from each person so it is likely comparisons can be made.

Disadvantages with semi-structured interviews

- The non-standardised method means questions are worded differently, so interviewees may interpret them differently.

- The interviewer's own biases may influence the phrasing of questions and the interpretation of answers.
- They are difficult to replicate (problems of reliability).
- They are unsystematic and vary from one individual to the next making comparisons difficult.

Advantages with structured open-ended interviews

- Exactly the same areas will be covered in all interviews.
- Data can be analysed more easily.
- They can be replicated.
- There is less room for interviewer bias to influence the results (although there can still be some, due for example to the tone of voice used by the interviewer).
- Several different interviewers can use the same interview schedule.
- Reliability of all types is higher.

Disadvantages with structured open-ended interviews

- There is no flexibility. If the interviewee raises interesting issues not on the list these will not be followed up.
- Answers may be less natural and interviewees feel less relaxed. When people know that they are being asked a set list of questions they may respond less fully.
- It may be difficult to code the answers given as they may vary widely from person to person.
- If the questions have not been well-piloted beforehand there may be misunderstandings.

Advantages with fully structured interviews

- They are quick and inexpensive to administer.
- They are easily replicated.
- Data analysis is easier.
- There is less chance for interpersonal bias to affect the results.
- There is high reliability of all kinds.

Disadvantages with fully structured interviews

- There is a great loss of richness in the data gathered. In more open-ended interviews the individual nuances in replies often reveal a great deal, and there is no room with closed questions for consideration of such differences.
- The interviewee is constrained as to the type of answer they can give: they may wish to say 'Sometimes' not 'Yes' or 'No'.
- Unless the questions have been carefully piloted, there may well be misunderstandings.
- Only *quantitative* data can be collected.
- There may be a problem of **response set** where the interviewee always says 'Yes' (or perhaps 'No') to each question. Questions have to be carefully phrased to try to counteract this problem.

How would you answer the following exam-type question?

1 Describe *two* different types of interviews.
2 What are the problems that arise when interpreting each type of interview?

(Some useful key words are: structure, comparability of results, ease of analysis, qualitative data, quantitative data, replicability, reliability, inter-rater reliability, interviewer bias, freedom for reply, response set.)

Exercise 13

Correlational research

The use of the cor*relatio*nal method (as its name suggests) refers to research which uses techniques which look at the relationship between two or more variables. For example is there a relationship between now big your feet are and how tall you are? or between how much alcohol you consume per week and your academic results?

When using correlational methods we investigate the extent to which changes in variables are related to each other. *We cannot and must not, however, assume that a change in one variable is responsible for causing changes in the other.* To take the last example given above, it *could* be your consumption of six pints of beer a night which is the cause of your low grades, but it *might be* your low grades which have driven you to drink. There could also be another factor – such as your distress at the fact that Baby Spice doesn't answer your letters – which has led to both your high consumption of beer and your low academic grades.

It is not possible to identify independent and dependent variables in correlational research – the researcher is not manipulating one variable and measuring the effect on another. Rather they are using statistics to see if there is any relationship between two variables.

You will sometimes find cases of the misrepresentation of the results of correlational research in the media. For example there is much debate over the relationship between violence in the media and aggression. There are correlational studies which show that people who watch a lot of violence are more aggressive. But does watching media violence *make* you more aggressive? or is it that aggressive people *like* to watch violence more than less aggressive people? or could some other factor (such as home background) be involved? Keep a critical lookout for such examples.

Studies may show a **positive correlation** (e.g. the greater number of gooseberry bushes in the garden, the more children in the family).

Other studies may show a **negative correlation** (e.g. the more frightened you are of dentists, the less frequently you visit them).

If there is no relationship (e.g. between the number of freckles you have and your IQ score) then the variables are said to be *uncorrelated* or *unrelated*.

Exercise 14

Are the following correlations positive or negative?

1 The hotter the weather, the more ice cream is sold.
2 The smaller the miniature pony, the greater its value.
3 The lower the prices, the more the shop sells.
4 The better behaved the child, the less they are punished.
5 The fewer the calories eaten, the less the weight.

Common uses of the correlational method

Correlation is commonly used in psychology:

- when the test/re-test *reliability* of a psychological test is being measured. If you take the test today and again next week, do you obtain similar scores?
- when **concordance rates** are calculated in twin studies. If one twin has blue eyes, what is the probability that the other twin will have blue eyes?
- when the relationship between a change that has already occurred over which the researcher had no control (an *ex post facto* change) and some present variable is being studied. An example might be a study on the relationship between how much you read as a child and your exam results at the age of sixteen.
- when a relationship is being studied which it would be unethical to manipulate experimentally. For example it would be unethical to raise a group of children watching only TV programmes containing violence to study if this made them more aggressive.

Advantages of the correlational method

- This technique allows a researcher to measure relationships between naturally occurring variables.
- Correlational studies can indicate trends which might then lead to further research using experimental means to establish any causal links.

Limitations of the correlational method

- The use of the correlational technique does not permit the investigator to draw conclusions about cause-and-effect relationships.
- It is very difficult to control extraneous variables which may influence the results.
- There may appear to be no relationship between variables when a correlational analysis is run, but there may actually be a *curvilinear relationship* between the variables. A **scattergram** will show this, which is one reason why it is very important that one is always drawn.

Details of the *interpretation* and *analysis* of correlational data are given in Section Nine later in the book.

1 Devise your own example of a positive correlation.
2 Devise your own example of a negative correlation.
3 Suppose that data was published that showed a strong negative correlation between the amount of television people watch at home and the number of car accidents they have. It is claimed that this shows that television must teach safe driving habits. Would you accept this explanation? Can you think of an alternative explanation for the findings?

Summary table of methods of investigation

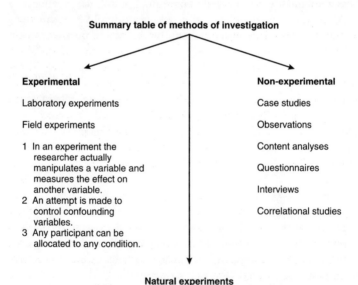

Experimental

Laboratory experiments

Field experiments

1 In an experiment the researcher actually manipulates a variable and measures the effect on another variable.
2 An attempt is made to control confounding variables.
3 Any participant can be allocated to any condition.

Non-experimental

Case studies

Observations

Content analyses

Questionnaires

Interviews

Correlational studies

Natural experiments
It is possible to identify an IV and a DV but, although a variable alters, this is not under the control of the researcher: it has changed due to real-life factors.

Quasi-experiments
It is possible to identify an IV and a DV but it is not possible to randomly allocate participants to conditions.

Qualitative and quantitative methods

As explained in the preliminaries, academic psychology has long emphasised the importance of the *scientific method*, as used in other natural sciences, and this has led to an emphasis on research which collects numerical data which is analysed statistically: the so-called **empirical** approach. The word *quantitative* is derived from the verb 'to quantify' which means to count or to assign a numerical value to things, and this approach is often referred to as *the quantitative paradigm*. An example is the work of Peterson and Peterson (1959) on memory for lists of nonsense syllables such as WID or HEQ, where the participants were asked to memorise such lists and then recall them immediately or after varying time delays. The researchers were interested in *how many* could be recalled. Another example would be the work of Asch (1955), in his famous study of conformity, when he counted *how many* participants conformed to incorrect answers that were given by 'stooges' on *how many* trials.

A second approach is referred to as *the qualitative paradigm*. A common thread running through all qualitative research is the identification of the participant's own subjective view of the situation or the identification of other people's subjective views of the participant's behaviour. This often involves detailed, open-ended analysis of verbal, written or visual material which is not converted into numerical scales. Those who favour this approach argue that qualitative methods are *context bound* (the findings are only meaningful in the context of the particular situation in which they were gathered). They argue that psychology should study the meaning of an event to the individual and that this meaning is *constructed* within the context of historical, social and cultural relationships. This approach is known as *constructivism* or *constructionism*. An example is Bartlett's work (1932) on memory for stories when instead of testing *how much* people could remember he studied *what* they recalled, and showed that this was distorted to fit the cultural experiences of the individual. Thus he found 'going to the river to hunt seals', which appeared in one story, was often changed to 'going fishing'. A more radical example is the work of Griffin (1985), who used semi-structured interviews, observations and case studies in a qualitative study of young girls' perceptions of the move from school to the job market. Griffin writes:

I was able to set young women's experiences in a cultural context....The use of qualitative methods did enable me to examine the impact of the cultural and social processes which were relevant for these women at a time of rising youth unemployment....I undertook the study from a (dynamic) feminist perspective.

(1995: 120)

You should realise that the differences in approach amongst those who argue for the use of qualitative methods are as widespread as those amongst practitioners of the more traditional empiricist approach. On the conservative boundary are those who emphasise the importance of gathering data on how the participant *perceives* and *interprets* the research situation when conducting research. At the radical extreme is the approach that shuns any experimentation and sees all social life as discourse or text.

When are qualitative or quantitative methods used?

The answer to this question is that it depends upon the nature of the research being conducted and the philosophical approach of the researcher.

If you are interested in whether memory for a tray containing thirty objects is more accurate if participants are hypnotised or not hypnotised, it makes sense to conduct a controlled experiment and to quantify the results. If you are interested in the experience of hypnosis to the participant, then you would use qualitative methods. Some researchers (e.g. Silverman 1977) have argued that a productive strategy is to use a mix of qualitative *and* quantitative methods in research studies. This idea is an established approach in other social sciences – those of you studying sociology will be familiar with the idea of 'triangulation' (the idea that in research we should compare at least two views of the topic; for example, we might compare data from an interview with data from naturalistic observation). This has led to the use of a greater diversity of methods, the collection of different types of data, and greater understanding of relative strengths and weaknesses.

Draw a table and organise the following points under the headings 'Most relevant to quantitative methods' and 'Most relevant to quali-tative methods'.

subjective/high reliability/unstructured design/naturalistic setting/objective/produce rich data/idiographic/structured design/artificial setting/nomothetic/low reliability/procedure is solely determined by the researcher/rigorous control/low comparability across studies/more realistic results.

Exercise 16

The analysis of qualitative data is dealt with in Section Fourteen.

Section Three

Designs used in research

The common designs used in psychological research are **independent groups**, **repeated measures**, **matched pairs**, **single participant**, **longitudinal**, **cross-sectional** and **cohort studies** (the latter three being most common in developmental psychology).

Do not confuse the method *used (experimental/non-experimental) with the* design *used.*

- *Independent groups design* (also called *independent measures*, *independent participants* and *between groups design*). Here there are two (or more) conditions in the research and there are different people being tested in each condition. For example in a memory experiment in one condition the group recalls words immediately and in the other condition the group recalls them the next day. *There are different individuals in each experimental condition.*

- *Repeated measures design* (also called *related measures, related samples* and *within groups design*). Here the same participants are tested in two (or more) different conditions. For example in a memory experiment the same people are asked to recall the list of words immediately and then again on the next day. *All participants perform in each experimental condition.*

- *Matched pairs design.* Here there are different participants in the different conditions, but they are carefully matched on variables which the researcher feels may affect performance in the experiment (for example age, IQ, gender, cultural background, etc.).

- *Single participant design.* Only one person is used in the experiment. This is uncommon but was used in some early research (for example Ebbinghaus' research [1885], when he intensively researched his own memory). It differs from a case study in that it uses the experimental method with variables being manipulated by the researcher.

Exercise 17

Identify the type of design used in these experiments:

1 Babies are shown two patterns and the difference in the time spent looking at each is recorded.
2 The differences in the perceptual ability of kittens raised in different environments is compared.
3 Twenty students are given an IQ test and then re-tested a month later after they have been given practice sessions to see if these improve their scores. The two sets of results are compared.
4 The reading ability of twenty ten-year-olds in a class of forty is compared with twenty ten-year-olds in a class of twenty-five. All attend inner-city schools, have been taught by similar reading methods and have similar IQs.
5 The length of visual after-effects in introverts and extroverts is compared.
6 The GCSE maths grades of girls and boys attending the same school are compared.

The advantages and disadvantages of different experimental designs

A useful way to consider this topic is to think about how the choice of design might affect the investigation of a hypothesis. For example, supposing you investigate whether there is a difference in the grades awarded to students who submit word-processed or handwritten essays,

- if you used an *independent groups design* you would have different students and thus different essays in the two conditions. How would this affect the results?
- if you used *repeated measures* each student's work would be in both conditions – in one case word-processed and in the other hand-written. Would this be better?
- in *matched pairs* you would have different students in the two groups but match them on usual grades obtained. Would this work?

In the above case an independent groups design would not work very well (it might be a possible choice if you had a very large sample), but any differences found could be due to the essays being of different standards.

Sometimes, however, an independent groups design would be the best choice. Consider this experiment: you decide to investigate conformity by showing participants fake written 'stooge' answers. People are asked how many beans there are in a jar – one group see (a) and another group see (b) – and are then asked to write down their own estimate.

| (a) | 40 | 42 | 40 | — | — |
| (b) | 70 | 68 | 70 | — | — |

Participants are told they are the fourth person you have asked. (The correct answer is actually 55.) In this case an independent measures design would work well. Could you use a repeated measures design? Why not?

Independent groups design

Advantages

- You don't have to worry about **order effects**.
- You can use exactly the same materials for each group.
- There is no need to leave a gap between testing the groups.

Disadvantages

- Participant variables are not controlled. You have different people in each condition and they may vary in important ways. You can try to eliminate this by the *random allocation* of participants to groups but this is not always possible and there is no guarantee it will work. For example if I was to compare the answers on an experimental design question from two different groups of students, one of whom read this book while the others read another textbook, and I found that the ones who read this book did better, the sad fact is that I could not be certain that this was due to the book – it could be because all the students who had the greatest understanding of experimental design were in that particular group.
- You will need twice as many participants as in a repeated measures design. For example if you want fifteen participants in each condition you will need two groups of fifteen (i.e. thirty people) instead of fifteen in total for repeated measures.

Repeated measures design

Advantages

- You have exactly the same participants in each group and so do not need to worry about the effect participant variables that you are not interested in may have on your results. If you used a repeated measures design when you were comparing speed in solving common or uncommon anagrams, you don't have to worry that some people in one group are better at solving anagrams than people in the other group. Everyone is in both groups.
- You don't need to find as many participants.

Disadvantages

- You may have problems with *order effects*. As each person does two or more tasks doing the first task might affect how well they do the second (e.g. in the anagram-solving experiment above, practice doing common anagrams might make you faster solving uncommon anagrams.) *To control for this you could use* **counterbalancing** (i.e. half the group do task A then task B whilst the rest do task B then task A). See Section Seven, p. 80, for more explanation.
- You may have to leave a gap between conditions because the participants get tired or bored. This might make the research longer and more complicated.
- You sometimes need different materials in each condition. If you use a repeated measures design in a memory experiment you can't keep asking people to learn the same words. It may, however, be difficult to produce comparable word lists.
- Participants may guess what the research is about as they compare the two conditions and so results are complicated by *demand characteristics*. (See Section Five, pp. 67–9)
- You may lose participants between tasks. If the first task was really boring they won't want to do the second!

Matched pairs design

Advantages

- There are no problems with order effects.
- There is no need to wait between testing groups.
- You can use the same materials for each group.

Disadvantages

- It is very time-consuming. It requires a lot of background research to find well-matched subjects.
- The loss of one person means the loss of a whole pair.
- However well you plan you are unlikely to be able to control all the variables that could affect the results, and the one missed may turn out to be important.

Single participant design

Advantage

- It is useful if a great deal of training is required.

Disadvantages

- It is not possible to generalise the results to other people.
- Your single participant might be an oddball!

Exercise 18

Give one advantage and one disadvantage for the use of the designs chosen in the following studies:

1 A repeated measures experiment to test the effect of hunger on the ability to solve anagrams about food.
2 A matched pairs experiment to compare the ability to solve anagrams shown by males and females.
3 An independent groups experiment to test the effects of practice on the ability to solve anagrams.

Design of studies in developmental psychology

All the previously mentioned designs may, of course, be used in developmental research but, in addition, three other types of design are often used to gather data about *age-related changes*. These are:

- longitudinal studies,
- cross-sectional studies, and
- cohort studies.

Longitudinal studies

In these the *same individuals* are studied over a period of time. For example Roger Brown studied the language development of the same three children over two years.

Advantages

- The individuals are compared with themselves. This controls for *participant variability*.
- It is the only sure way to study the long-term effects of factors affecting upbringing. In a longitudinal study data is collected *at the time that events occur* and so there is no reliance on retrospective data which is often flawed or biased.

Disadvantages

- It takes a long time and thus is expensive.
- Participants may drop out or be hard to find in the later stages. This can raise problems of low participant numbers and of test/re-test reliability if the final sample is not really comparable with the initial sample.
- It is difficult to replicate.

Longitudinal designs are a kind of repeated measures design, and so share some of the same advantages and disadvantages.

Cross-sectional studies

This design compares individuals of different ages on their performance on some task. For example many studies have compared the intellectual development of children of different ages: perhaps using a group of twenty four-year-olds, a group of twenty eight-year-olds and a group of twenty twelve-year-olds.

Advantages

- It is much quicker than a longitudinal study.
- It can be easily replicated.
- It can identify differences between age groups which could then be studied more intensively – perhaps using a longitudinal design.

Disadvantages

- The difference between the age groups observed could be due to confounding variables, not to the variable under investigation. For example eight-year-olds will have been attending school for three years whilst four-year-olds may not even have been to a playgroup or nursery.
- Cross-sectional studies tell us nothing about the development *within* individuals.
- Cohort effects can occur. This refers to the fact that people born at different times will have had distinct life experiences and so any differences between the age groups may well be nothing to do with age itself. If I was to compare people aged seventy and people aged twenty in 1998, the former have lived through a world war, have probably married, had children, worked for many years, etc., whilst the latter are less likely to have done any of these. So are differences – perhaps in moral attitudes – related to age differences? or would similar differences be found between two groups of twenty-year-olds with as different life experiences?

Cross-sectional studies are a type of independent groups design, and so share some of the same advantages and disadvantages.

Cohort studies

Here a number of people from different cross sections of age groups are followed for a number of years. An example would be if you studied a group of three-year-olds for five years, a group of eight-year-olds for five years and a group of thirteen-year-olds for five years.

Thus in the space of this five-year period you would have studied ages three to eighteen.

This has the advantage of covering a wide age-range quickly, but the disadvantage that there is no control of:

- participant variables, and
- different life experiences.

If I was to carry out the above study in 1998 the three-year-olds would have been born in 1995 and will not be eighteen until 2013; their life experiences will not be the same as the thirteen-year-olds born in 1985 who would be eighteen in 2003 – think how fast society changes.

1 If you were going to conduct a twenty-year longitudinal study on the effects of divorce on children why would it be very important to do a pilot study first?

2 Explain why participant variability can be problematic in a cross-sectional study.

3 What is meant by a 'cohort effect'?

4 Give one advantage and one disadvantage that a longitudinal study has over a cohort study.

Exercise 19

Section Four

Sampling

Having decided on your aim and hypotheses you will need to decide who you are going to study and how you will select them – or in other words who your sample will be. (You must, of course, also consider **sampling** if you are studying non-human animals or carrying out a content analysis.)

First decide which group (or *target population*) you are interested in. The term *target population* is used to mean 'all the members of the group in which you are interested'. Thus the nature of the target population depends on your research. If you want to compare the height of six-year-old girls and six-year-old boys, then your target population will be all six-year-olds. If you want to investigate attitudes to psychology among biology teachers, then your target population would be all biology teachers.

You should be clear on the difference between the target population and population in general. For example an exam question asked students to identify the target population in Milgram's obedience study (1963). As Milgram recruited his participants by placing an advert in a newspaper in the USA, the target population would be all those who read the advert – not all Americans.

It is generally impossible to test everyone in your target population and so you must select a sample group of participants to represent the target population.

Exercise 20

Identify the target population in the following studies:

1 A comparison of male and female reading habits.
2 A test to see if nine out of ten cats *do* prefer Whiskas.
3 A study into whether cat owners believe the Whiskas advert.
4 Research into the effectiveness of the use of cognitive therapy for agoraphobia.
5 An investigation into play in one-year-old infants.

Methods of choosing a sample

As stated above, you are selecting a sample to represent the total population. You should try, therefore, to avoid choosing an unrepresentative or **biased sample** as this can invalidate your results. For example an early political opinion poll in the USA was conducted by telephone – but the pollsters had forgotten that at that time only wealthy people had phones. The results were very inaccurate!

There are several ways of choosing a sample from the target population:

Random sampling is ideal as it should be unbiased, but it is rarely used in psychology as it is time-consuming to select a sample in this way and thus is expensive. To select a random sample you identify everyone in the target population and then select the number of participants you need in a way that gives everyone in the population an equal chance of being picked. For example, you could give them all a number and then select the sample required using random number tables or you could put all the names in a bag and pick out however many you need.

The important thing to remember is that in a random sample every member of the target population has an equal chance of being selected.

Opportunity sampling is a popular method. This involves selecting the first people you meet who fit the right criteria, who you are prepared to ask to help and who are prepared to help you. Opportunity sampling can produce a biased sample as it is easy for the researcher to approach people from their own social and cultural group. It is easy for you to use your friends and family in your research, but are they really representative of your target population?

Despite such problems opportunity sampling is widely used in psychological research – possibly because it is quick, easy and inexpensive. It is perfectly adequate when investigating processes which are assumed to work in a similar way in all 'normal' individuals – for example work on some areas of cognitive psychology.

If you are doing a natural experiment (i.e. one in which the independent variable is changed by some factor outside your control) you may have to use an opportunity sample. For example if your research were on the effects of Caesarean births, you would have no control over which babies were born in this way and there might be such a small number that you would use all of them.

Random sampling and opportunity sampling are not the same thing

To test twenty people from your college using random sampling you would have to get a list of the names of everyone attending, give them all a number, pick out twenty numbers and then go and find those twenty people.

To test twenty people from your college using opportunity sampling you probably ask the first twenty people you meet.

They are very different methods!

Systematic sampling is another method for choosing a sample. Here every eighth, fifteenth or hundredth (or whatever) member of the target population is selected. For example if you had a class register and picked out every third name, you would be using systematic sampling. If you decide every third person is to be asked you have to include these people in your sample, whoever they are. In this way systematic sampling does overcome the bias of the researcher that can occur with opportunity sampling. However, the participants are not selected at random as it is not the case that all have an equal chance of inclusion in the sample. Systematic sampling is *reasonably* quick and easy, at least with a small target population, and can be a useful method to use.

Stratified sampling on the other hand is time-consuming and difficult, but should lead to a sample which is an accurate representation of the target population. Here each relevant variable in the total population must be considered. For example what percentage are male? female? over sixty? under sixteen? studying A-level maths? middle class? born in England?

This method may be used by opinion pollsters who select a relatively small sample to represent the whole electorate. This sample must be representative of the whole electorate in terms of age, gender, occupation, etc. if it is to be of use: e.g. if 1 per cent of the electorate are professional females under twenty-five years old, then 1 per cent of the sample must be professional females under twenty-five.

Quota sample In a stratified sample the participants are randomly selected from within these criteria. A **quota sample** is similar, but here the participants are selected by opportunity sample from within the criteria. This method is often used in market research as it is quicker and cheaper than stratified sampling. The market researcher is told to interview twenty male white-collar workers and twenty female manual workers but can select these by opportunity sample. Thus it is open to some of the same biases as this latter method. For example the researcher might ask twenty women who all work for the same company.

Self-selected sample A **self-selected sample** (or volunteer sample) is sometimes used and may be chosen in two ways:

- Participants may be *volunteers* replying to an advertisement. (A famous example of this is the study on obedience by Milgram [1963] which was mentioned earlier.) It is necessary to be wary of possible bias. Perhaps some types of people may be more likely to volunteer than others and perhaps volunteers may be particularly keen to please the experimenter.
- Participants may be *self-selected* in that they are passing a particular spot at a certain time. For example if you are investigating whether car drivers stop at a zebra crossing, the sample is self-selected as it consists of the people who happen to be driving there at that time. (The researchers have to rely on taking whoever is driving along the road.)

Snowball sample   Finally a **snowball sample** is sometimes used. This often applies when it is difficult to find participants. For example if you were researching heroin addiction, you might start with one person and ask them for the name of another addict, and so on so that the sample 'snowballs'. With some populations this might be the only way to find participants.

List one advantage and one disadvantage for each type of the following types of sampling:

Random   Quota
Opportunity   Snowball
Stratified   Self-selected
Systematic

Exercise 21

Sample size

Having chosen a sampling method you next have to decide on the *size of your sample*. It is difficult to give a definite answer here as it depends on the *size of the target population*, the *resources* available to the researcher, the *sampling method chosen* and so on.

61

- First, if statistical tests are to be used there are often minimum requirements. For example a 2×2 chi-square test is less reliable if you have under twenty participants.
- Second, it depends upon the size of the target population. If this is everyone eligible to vote in a general election then you need a larger sample than if it is everyone eligible to vote in a local election. You want a large enough sample to be truly representative – but remember results from thirty participants carefully chosen at random or by systematic sampling might be more meaningful than those of a hundred people chosen by opportunity sampling in a pub. Size is not everything!
- A third factor is the importance of the research. If the results are going to be used for policy-making then you would need to be as sure as possible that your answers were correct, and you would need a larger sample than for something like coursework.
- Finally, sample size will depend on the time and resources available.

The size of sample used in psychology is usually a compromise between these factors. In general use as large a sample as you can *remembering that a large sample is not a cure for poor experimental design and biased sampling.*

For experimental work investigating an independent variable that probably affects everyone (e.g. memory processing) a sample of twenty-five to thirty is usually considered large enough even for research which is published in journals. In coursework you can use a few less: perhaps fifteen or so for a repeated measures design and thirty (split into two groups) for an independent groups design. In other types of coursework research, such as observational studies or clinical interviews, it may not be practical to use as many participants. In a questionnaire study you might use more.

1 Explain the difference between a random sample and an opportunity sample.
2 Why might replies from a sex questionnaire published in *Playboy* be unreliable? What kind of sample would this be?
3 List three factors that influence the choice of sample size used in research.
4 You investigate why students at your college choose certain academic subjects for study. How would you select:

- a random sample of fifty?
- a stratified sample of fifty?
- a quota sample of fifty?
- an opportunity sample of fifty?

Exercise 22

Section Five

The experiment as a social situation

Much psychological research involves people. This makes the conduct of research much more complex than work in the natural sciences. If you mix copper sulphate and sulphuric acid the molecules do not sit in the test-tube wondering why you have done this and what you are hoping to prove. If you deprive a plant of light it doesn't think: 'A-ha!…photosynthesis experiment. What shall I do this time?' People are *reflexive* – they consider what you are doing and why.

Researchers are people too: some are nice and some are not so nice; some rate highly on attractiveness scales and some do not; some follow procedures exactly and some do not.

All these things can affect the results.

Experimenter bias

Experimenters can affect the results of psychological research in several ways. Barber (1976) suggests that the following factors can affect results:

- *Failing to follow standardised procedures or instructions.* The effects of this are self-explanatory.
- *Misrecording results.* The effects of such carelessness are again obvious.
- *'Fudging' results in some way.* The best known example of this is probably Cyril Burt's research on concordance rates of IQ in twins (1958), where there are claims that allegedly scores were altered or invented.
- *Personal attributes.* As mentioned above researchers will differ in gender, appearance, race, manner, accent, and so on. The response to a large, male Scot might be different to the response to a shapely, female Italian.
- *Expectancy effects.* This refers to the clues that an experimenter may unintentionally give to participants about what the research is about and how they expect them to behave.

Suppose you ran an experiment with the hypothesis that women will prefer pictures of landscape with people in to those with no people in. You show the pictures in pairs, but unintentionally look disappointed every time a participant chooses a picture with no people in but look pleased each time they choose one with people. Your behaviour may act as a social reinforcement which affects the choices made.

Support comes from Rosenthal (1966). He gave students rats labelled 'maze bright' or 'maze dull' to test to see how quickly they learnt a maze. The rats were actually no different from each other, but differences were found between them that fitted the labels given! In some way the rats' behaviour was influenced by the expectations of the students running the experiment.

Another example is from early work on IQ in twins. Kamin (1974) claims that in Shields' study (1962), in some cases, Shields tested both twins in a pair himself and obtained a difference of scores of 8.5 IQ points. In the case of other twin pairs, testing was by two independent examiners and the difference was 22.4 IQ points. Kamin concludes 'there is clearly a strong suggestion that unconscious experimenter expectation may have influenced these results' (Kamin 1974: 74).

How might experimenter effects have influenced the results of the following studies:

1 A male interviewer asks women about pregnancy.
2 An observer stands by a zebra crossing watching how children cross the road.
3 A very attractive woman conducts a study into how long people can keep their arm in ice-cold water.
4 A teacher and a school sixth-former conduct interviews about how much homework sixth-formers do each week.

Exercise 23

Participant expectations and demand characteristics

Psychological research on human beings suffers the unavoidable problem that it is dealing with living, sentient creatures. People do not behave like robots. As soon as you ask them to help with your psychology coursework thoughts may enter their heads such as 'Freud...sex...'.

Psychological research (such as an experiment, interview, case study, etc.) is a social situation and, just as in any social situation, the participants will try to interpret what is happening. They may try to guess what is being investigated, what the researcher is expecting them to do, what the researcher hopes to prove, and so on. They will then decide whether to go along with this or not! This is what causes the problem. Participants may react in one of four ways:

- *The unaffected participant.* These try to behave as naturally as possible.
- *The ultra-helpful participant.* These try to work out what you hope they will do so that they can be really helpful and do it. They may even ask, 'What do you want me to do'!
- *The bloody-minded participant.* These try to work out what you hope they will do so that they can do the opposite or they give

patently silly replies. They are usually recognisable by the evil grin they give you.

- *The nervous participant.* They are so overcome by the fact they are taking part in research that they panic and behave quite out of character.

Of course, you only really want the first group in your research...but how do you know where to find them? The answer is you don't, and you will inevitably ask members of the second, third and fourth groups. Orne (1962) coined the phrase 'demand characteristics' to describe aspects of the research situation that prompt the participants to interpret what is happening in the research in a certain way, so that they then alter their behaviour in a way that seems to them to be appropriate. Cardwell states: 'By adjusting their behaviour to what they see as the "demands" of the experiment, participants introduce a bias that may contaminate the results of the study' (1996: 67).

Orne became interested in this area when researching hypnosis. He wanted to devise a really pointless task, reasoning that people would only continue to carry out such a task for a long time if they were hypnotised. He gave people a sheet of sums to calculate. When they finished the first sheet they were told to tear it into eight pieces, throw it away and then to do the next sheet. This was to continue until they protested. However, Orne found that some non-hypnotised participants continued for ages – one for over two hours, by which time the *researchers* were so bored watching him they told him to stop. When asked why he went on for so long the participant replied that it was obviously a test of perseverance and he was determined to get a high score! In other words his whole behaviour was affected by his own interpretation of the situation he was in.

Participants will be affected by:

- their surroundings,
- the researcher's characteristics,
- the researcher's behaviour, and
- their interpretation of what is going on in the situation.

A well-designed experiment will try to minimise these factors as much as possible.

- It might be best to keep the environment as natural as possible (given that there may be important confounding variables that need to be controlled) so that the effect of surroundings is minimised.
- Perhaps different experimenters should be used to see if they obtain similar results.
- Experimenters must be carefully trained so that they follow standardised procedures and do not communicate their expectations.
- Qualitative data can be obtained at the end of the research by asking participants what they thought was happening and how this affected their behaviour.

One famous experiment often criticised on the grounds of demand characteristics is Bandura's 'Bobo'-doll study (Bandura, Ross and Ross 1963). In one experiment he brought children into the university, showed them a film of an adult ill-treating an inflatable toy doll, and then placed the child in the situation that they had just seen in the film. The children imitated the adult. But do you think that they thought that this was what they were supposed to do? (The experiment shows that children *can* learn by imitation – but can the findings be generalised to real-life media viewing?)

This is one area where it might be useful to collect some qualitative data from your participants after you have finished testing them. Why not ask what they thought the study was about or ask why they answered as they did? Their answers could provide interesting data on demand characteristics.

Reducing bias

Many types of bias are very difficult to eradicate and it is very important that researchers are sensitive to such issues when they plan their research.

A variety of methods are sometimes used, two of which are:

- the single blind procedure
- the double blind procedure

With the **single blind procedure** the participants may know what the research is about, but they don't know which group they themselves are in. If you were testing whether extra vitamin C reduces the severity of colds, you could make the details of the research known to your participants. If they think it worthwhile, they are more likely to cooperate fully. You could tell them there will be two groups – one receiving a tablet of one gram of vitamin C a day and the other receiving a placebo tablet identical in appearance and taste. They will not know which group they will be in and thus you should have controlled for participant expectations.

It is still possible, however, that the *researcher* may behave in a slightly different way when giving out the tablets if they know which is which. This can be controlled by using the **double blind procedure**. Here the person giving out the tablets doesn't know which bottle contains which tablet. They know they must give one group of people Bottle A and the other Bottle B, but not which bottle contains the vitamin C and which the placebo. Only a researcher removed from the actual research situation knows which is which. This means that there should be control over both participant expectations and **experimenter bias**.

Another thing that researchers sometimes do in an attempt to stop participants guessing what the research is about is to use **deception**. This, of course, raises ethical issues as the participants will not have given their full, informed consent before taking part, but it is not uncommon to find deception used – especially if revealing the true nature of the research will obviously affect a participant's response. For example Asch (1955), in his work on conformity, said that he was investigating the perception of line-length. It was obviously not possible to tell people he was studying conformity and expect that they would behave naturally. The extent to which such ruses are successful is debatable. (For more discussion on this point see Section Eight, which includes more on ethical issues.)

1   Explain how you would devise research including the use of the single blind procedure to test whether the use of a special drink *Memorade* improves exam performance.

2   Explain how you would devise an experiment using the double blind procedure to test whether massaging sprains with new improved *Spraineze* or old *Spraineze* best aids recovery.

Exercise 24

Section Six

- Reliability
- Validity

Reliability

This is a crucial area in all empirical research. (It is not always so important in qualitative research which may not, by its very nature, be replicable.) It is important that any results that are obtained can be *replicated* if the work is repeated by someone else, as a measure needs to produce *consistent* results if the findings are to be generalised beyond the original research. If this is the case (that is if a result can be repeated), the measure is said to be *reliable*.

Methods of measuring reliability

The issue of reliability is applied to various issues in psychology, for example the question of whether different judges or scorers agree with each other (inter-rater reliability) and the question of whether psychological tests give consistent findings.

Inter-rater reliability (also called *inter-judge* or *inter-scorer reliability*) is concerned with how closely different people who are measuring the same thing agree with each other. If agreement is high then inter-rater reliability is said to have been achieved.

If three teachers marked multiple choice exam answers there would probably be very close agreement between them: *inter-marker reliability* would be high. However, if they marked exactly the same essay in three different versions: word-processed, in neat writing or in near illegible writing then agreement might be lower: inter-marker reliability would be lower.

Inter-rater reliability is a particularly important issue in *observational research* or *content analysis*. No-one can have much confidence in the results unless two or more raters agree as to what is occurring.

Test reliability can be measured in three ways:

- *Test/re-test reliability.* The same group of people are given the same test twice and the correlation between their scores on each occasion is calculated. If the correlation is high and positive then there is said to be good test/re-test reliability.
- *Split-half reliability.* This is a measure of the internal consistency of a test. For example if you compare the score someone obtains on the even-numbered questions to that obtained on the odd-numbered questions is it similar? If it is then split-half reliability would be high.
- *Equivalent form reliability.* Sometimes there are two different versions of the same test. (For example Eysenck's Personality Inventory has two versions, Form A and Form B.) To test equivalent form reliability I would give you both versions and see if you got the same scores on both of them. If you did then equivalent form reliability would be high.

It is very important that research findings should be replicable or reliable and that psychometric tests should have high reliability.

1 Give two ways in which you could check whether your lecturer's essay-marking is reliable.
2 Every time *Neighbours* begins your dog indicates that it wants to go out. Explain whether this is a reliable finding.
3 You devise a questionnaire on attitudes to the idea of a single European currency. How could you check its reliability?

Validity

It is important that in any kind of research we are actually measuring what we think we are measuring. There are three aspects to this issue of **validity**: **internal validity**, **external validity** and **test validity**.

Internal validity

Is the effect that is observed in research really due to the manipulation of the independent variable?

For example, a researcher conducts an experiment using an independent groups design on people's ability to solve anagrams under very noisy or very quiet conditions. They find that performance is better in the noisy condition. However, is this difference due to the manipulation of the independent variable (noise level) or was there some uncontrolled variable or design flaw which produced the difference that was observed? Perhaps participant variables were not controlled and all the people in the noisy group were skilled anagram-solvers; or perhaps conditions of testing were not fully standardised and the 'noise group' were tested at a different time of day to the 'quiet group'?

Such problems would throw doubt on the internal validity of the research.

External validity

Even if we are confident that the research findings have internal validity, can the findings be applied to other groups of people, other situations or people tested at different historical times?

75

Whether or not the results can be generalised to other groups of people has been called 'population validity' by Bracht and Glass (1968). They refer to the issue of whether the results can be generalised to other situations as a problem of ecological validity. *Ecological validity refers to the extent to which the findings of a study can be generalised to other situations beyond the setting of that study.* A laboratory study may well be low in ecological validity because the same results might not be found in a more natural setting. Thus a study in which participants are asked to memorise a list of trigrams, such as FEP and KUV, does not necessarily tell us anything about memory in a real-life setting – such as recall of a shopping list. However, just because a study is conducted in a naturalistic setting does not automatically mean that it has high ecological validity. Piliavin, Rodin and Piliavin (1969) conducted a well-known study on helping behaviour in the real-life setting of a New York subway carriage. But are their results generalisable to other settings? Would they have found the same results on a bus in rural Devon?

A study only possesses ecological validity if the findings can be shown to apply to other situations outside the one in which the study was conducted.

Test validity

This refers to whether a test is measuring what it is supposed to measure.

Examples

It is quite possible for a test to be reliable but not valid – or to be valid but not reliable. If I timed how long you could stand on one leg I would probably get consistent (and thus *reliable*) results. However, you would not accept this as a *valid* measure of your intelligence. (Well…you might do if you balanced for a long time!)

If I gave you a psychometric test of aggression and you got a low score on the first occasion but, before I tested you again, you went home and had a terrific argument with your parents, you might get a high score on the second occasion that you took the test. This does not mean it is not a *valid* measure of aggression (indeed it seems to be a good one) but the results would certainly not be *reliable*.

Test validity can be measured in five main ways:

- **Face validity** simply refers to whether the test looks right to the eye of an independent observer. In the example before, standing on one leg lacks face validity as a measure of intelligence.
- **Concurrent validity** is a comparison of the test results and some other independent measure of the same variable measured *at around the same time*. You would expect there to be agreement between a test of mathematical aptitude given just before you took a maths exam and the exam result. If there was high agreement then there would be good concurrent validity.
- **Predictive validity** is a measure of whether the test results are a good predictor of *future* performance. Is a mathematical aptitude score obtained when you are eleven a good predictor of perform-ance in a maths exam at the age of sixteen? If the answer is 'Yes' then there is high predictive validity.
- **Content validity**. Do the items in the test cover the area of concern in a fair way? Are all areas covered in reasonably equal depth? It is obviously important that exam papers should have high content validity so that all areas of the syllabus are represented.
- **Construct validity**. Does the test measure some underlying construct? For example, do the numerical, verbal and spatial puzzles of many IQ tests actually measure intelligence as defined by their author?

The issue of validity arises in research as well as in testing. When you carry out a research project you should try to ensure you are using a valid measure. A popular practical (although one that raises some complex ethical issues) is a replication of the 'matching hypothesis', when participants are asked to independently rate the attractiveness of various husbands and wives and these ratings are then correlated. (The matching hypothesis suggests that people marry others of similar physical attractiveness to themselves.) However, students often take photographs from the local paper, cut them in half thereby removing someone's ear, photocopy them so they are vague blobs and *then* ask for ratings of attractiveness. Is this a valid measure of that person's attractiveness? Of course not.

The issues of reliability and validity apply to *questionnaire* and *interview* studies too. Unless there are exceptional circumstances you would expect people to give similar answers to a questionnaire or in an interview if they were questioned twice. Questions should also be phrased so that they are actually measuring what they are supposed to measure, and have good face validity.

1 Every time 'Neighbours' comes on the TV your dog indicates that it wants to go out. Is it valid to conclude it hates the programme?
2 How could you test whether exam results obtained at the age of eighteen are valid predictors of degree grades?
3 Explain why a measure of anxiety could be valid but not reliable.
4 Explain why an IQ test might be reliable but not valid.

Section Seven

Controlling variables

When research is planned it is obviously important that as many factors as possible which are not actually being studied but which might influence the results are controlled or eliminated. For instance, if you are studying memory it would not be sensible to test some people at 9 PM in a hot, noisy room and others at 9 AM in a peaceful, comfortable setting. You would want to control factors – such as noise level and time of day – which could affect people's memory.

A problem that can arise, however, is that if a situation is controlled really strictly, it becomes so artificial that it is unlikely that any results obtained can be generalised to other settings: that is it lacks *ecological validity*. For example, in much research on memory the familiarity of words is controlled by using nonsense syllables (HYJ, GEK, RIW, etc.) instead of real words. But how often do you learn such trigrams in real life? There are useful things that can be learnt from such controlled studies, but the lack of ecological validity must be borne in mind.

Standardisation of procedures in research

Two controls that are used in just about all research are the use of **standardised procedures** and **instructions**. The use of *standardised procedures* means that in every step of the research all participants are treated in an identical way and so all have the same experiences. Even small variations in procedures may affect participants in unforeseen ways. The use of standardised procedures can sometimes help to control *demand characteristics*, as all participants will have the same experience, and will also help to control for *experimenter bias* as all the researchers involved will follow the same procedures.

Standardised instructions, that is using identical instructions for all participants, are used for the same reasons.

Counterbalancing

Counterbalancing is a control for the *order effects* which can occur when participants do more than one activity in a research study. In any *repeated measures design* participants will do at least two tasks and it could well be the case that completing the first task affects performance on the second. This is known as an order effect, and occurs when *performing one task affects the performance of the next task*.

Example

If you were researching the equivalent form reliability of an intelligence test (i.e. whether participants obtain similar scores on the two forms of the test), you might ask participants to complete Test A and then complete Test B. However, the completion of the first test could affect how well they do on the second. People might be tired after the first test; alternatively there could be a **practice effect** which means they do the second test better. The way to control for this is by *counterbalancing* so that half the participants complete Test A and then do Test B, while the other half do Test B then Test A.

How would you counterbalance the presentation of material in the following repeated measures designs?

1 Participants are tested to see if they prefer *Coca Cola* or *Pepsi*.
2 In a study of the accuracy of marking, five examiners are asked to mark the same two essays.
3 In a test of Freudian sexual symbolism a group of students are asked to think of names for cartoon drawings of a triangle and a circle:

Exercise 27

Confounding variables

A *confounding variable* is something – other than the independent variable – which alters as you carry out research and which influences the results you get. Put more formally, *a confounding variable is anything which may unintentionally affect the dependent variable in the research being carried out.*

- Such confounding variables may act in a *constant* way on a group of participants, in which case they are called *constant errors...*
- or they can affect participants in a *random* fashion in which case they are called *random errors.*

Constant errors

If you test one group of people on a sunny day and the next group when it is raining, this would be a *constant error*. If you are researching whether men are more likely to help a girl in a long skirt who drops her books or the same girl in a short skirt, and it is good weather the day she has the long skirt on and bad weather when she has the short skirt on, you might be suprised to find she is helped more when she has the long skirt on – but this result has come about because of the confounding variable of the weather and is nothing to do with the skirt length!

Constant errors such as this are very serious and can lead to spurious conclusions. If you study the work on the biochemistry of schizophrenia, you will find there is a history of mistakes due to constant errors. In one study it was found that schizophrenics had lower iodine levels than a control group and so it was hypothesised that there was a link between low iodine levels and schizophrenia. Then it was later discovered that the schizophrenics (who were all at one hospital) had a diet low in iodine. Poor food was the constant error responsible for the findings.

Random errors

Random errors occur when variables change in a way that is beyond the control of the researcher but that affects participants in a random fashion. These are called *random variables*. For example, one participant is feeling ill, another has forgotten their glasses, a third has just had a row with someone, and so on. Such things affecting single participants are not usually considered serious as they probably even themselves out over the course of the research.

One technique a researcher might use to try to reduce random errors is to randomly allocate the participants to the conditions. This is not foolproof as very odd distributions can occur in a random selection but it does help to control for some potential sources of bias.

1 What is meant by the following terms: random errors, constant errors, order effects, counterbalancing, confounding variables, standardised instructions, standardised procedures.

2 A researcher runs an experiment – using a repeated measures design – on memory for two film clips, Clip A involving a car crash and Clip B involving Lassie rescuing a boy from drowning.

   (a) Name a random error which could occur and suggest how this could be controlled.

   (b) Name a constant error that could occur and suggest how this could be controlled.

   (c) In what order would you choose to show the films?

Exercise 28

Section Eight

Ethnocentric, cultural and androcentric biases

Ethnocentric bias occurs when only one ethnic group is used in the sample and yet it is assumed that generalisations can be made about other groups.

Cultural bias occurs when only one culture (or subculture) is sampled and yet it is assumed that we can generalise from this culture to other cultures.

Androcentric bias occurs when only males are studied.

There has been a tendency in psychology to regard the behaviour of present-day, white westerners as 'normal' and capable of forming the basis for generalisations about *all* human behaviour. To make matters worse, it is often the implicit assumption that our own cultural or ethnic group is actually superior to others.

In work on child-rearing practices it sometimes seems to be the assumption that what sociologists call the 'cornflake-packet family' of husband, wife and children is the norm and is the 'best' way to bring up children. This is despite the fact that family structures vary from culture to culture and also within cultures. For example there have been great changes in family structures in western society over the last 200 years, related to factors such as industrialisation and increased geographical mobility. What is the norm in present-day Britain or America was not the norm 50 or 250 years ago, and is not necessarily the norm in other countries, yet is too often seen as a standard against which to judge other ways to rear children.

To make things even worse, many studies widely quoted in textbooks have used only males in their sample and it is still true that the majority of lecturers and researchers in psychology are men. It is argued by many feminists, for example Griffin (1991), that men's subjective experiences will necessarily reflect their position as members of the dominant social group. If you study moral development you will meet Gilligan's criticisms (1982) of Kohlberg's book describing research into the stages of moral development (1969). Kohlberg interviewed boys as to how they would behave if faced with certain moral dilemmas and devised stages of development based on justice and logic. Gilligan argues that his findings have a gender bias against girls who, she argues, base their moral reasoning on caring and personal relationships. The point at issue here for the present discussion is not who was right, but rather that Kohlberg assumed he could generalise from his research on boys to girls as well.

Yet another bias is that many studies have used undergraduates as the participants. Valentine (1982) estimated that 75 per cent of British and American research draws on this population. I would not want to argue that undergraduates are an *abnormal* group – I was once one myself – but they do form a biased population in terms of age, class and education. Will they react in the same way as old-age pensioners, for example?

The problems that arise from these biases become clear if we look at research in social psychology. Is it really possible to assume that the findings from the white American male undergraduates tested by Asch in his work on conformity can be generalised to middle-aged Chinese women? Such a generalisation *may* turn out to be accurate – but it should not be assumed to be the case. There are several studies (see Berry *et al.* 1992) which show that conformity varies from culture to culture. Some cultures emphasise independence, others value working together and compliance. The work of Kohn (1969) has shown these differences even occur between different social classes in the United States.

You should consider the possible ethnocentric and cultural biases in your own research and how this limits the conclusions that you can draw.

Ethical issues in research

When you design a research study you should ask yourself whether you yourself would really want to take part as a participant. In psychology we are dealing with other living creatures; you should treat them with respect.

You may be familiar with the famous examples that books frequently discuss – such as Milgram's 'shocking' experiment or Zimbardo *et al.*'s 'prison' experiment. You might think, however, that your own research is so different from these examples that you don't really need to worry about ethics. After all you're not likely to lock people in prison, are you?

Perhaps some examples closer to home – from A-level coursework – might show how easy it is to treat people disrespectfully. How would you have felt if you had been a participant in these coursework studies?

- Two sixth formers rated a class of thirteen- to fourteen-year-olds as to how 'attractive' they were.
- Schoolgirls waiting for their BCG injections were led to believe it would be very painful and shown a giant syringe that they were told would be used.
- Eleven- to twelve-year-olds were given a questionnaire by two sixth formers about their feelings towards step-parents.

Is it really ethical to do this sort of study ?

The ethics of research using human and non-human animals began to be seriously discussed in the 1960s and since then ethical codes of conduct have been drawn up. These will only be summarised here – you should consult a book on perspectives in psychology for more details[1] – but you must consider ethical issues when you design coursework projects.

When conducting research on human beings the main points to consider are as follows:

- Participants should give fully *informed consent* before taking part in research. If your research involves children under the age of sixteen you should also have the consent of their parents or an adult *in loco parentis*. (This does not mean you ask a teacher *instead* of the schoolchildren. You should ask the children for consent as well, if they are old enough to understand.)
- Participants should not be *deceived* about the purpose of the study. However, problems sometimes arise when the reaction of participants would be affected if they knew what the study is actually about. For example, in a study on perceptual set you cannot really explain to your participants that your aim is to investigate whether an ambiguous figure is seen as a rat or as a man – they will then be looking for both figures!
- In all such cases participants should be fully *debriefed* when you have finished testing them. You will probably find that in cases of minor deception no one will object. *However, if people do object you should stop the research.* It is also important that debriefing should occur as soon as possible – participants do not like to feel that they have gone away with a false idea of what the research was about.
- You should make it clear that people can *withdraw* from the study at any time or refuse to allow their data to be used.
- You should not expose participants to *risk* or *stress*. This includes being sensitive to cultural issues. A study on the perception of swear-words might not seem stressful to you but it might be to your granny!
- All results should be kept *confidential* and participants should not be referred to by name in reports.
- If you are doing an observational study you may well not be able to ask for the informed consent of participants or be able to debrief them afterwards. In such cases the guidelines say that you should

1 See, for example, Mike Cardwell's book in this series, *Ethical Issues in Psychology*.

only observe people in situations when they would expect their behaviour to be seen by strangers. In such studies it is important not to intrude into people's *privacy* and you should be sensitive to cultural differences.

- Another important issue is that you should not claim *competence* that you don't possess. Just because you have studied anxiety disorders doesn't mean you can set up as a therapist! You must carefully consider whether you really do have the competence to undertake research into areas where specialist knowledge is needed. Are you really competent to carry out a case study on mental health or to interview people about delicate personal issues?

- Most importantly you must not claim to be able to diagnose or offer advice to people on psychological issues unless you possess the necessary *professional qualifications*.

The deception dilemma

What should you do if your proposed study involves deceiving participants?

- You can explain what you are proposing to do to other people from similar social and cultural backgrounds to the population that you are intending to study and see if they would be prepared to take part. This would give you an indication of likely reactions.

- You must fully debrief people at the end of the research. If people object then you should stop. The debriefing should occur as soon as you have finished testing each person. A survey by Dellerba and Hodges (1998) found that people said they didn't mind minor deception as long as it was explained to them *as soon as a study was completed*, but that they thought they would feel they had been made fools of if things were explained later.

- You must allow people to withdraw from the study if they wish to do so or allow them to withdraw their data at the end.

Exercise 29

What ethical problems are raised by the following studies?

1 Sixth formers stop eleven- and twelve-year-olds in the school corridor and ask them to guess how many beans there are in a jar. Half are given a piece of paper to write on which appears to have three high estimates already on it and half are given some paper with three low estimates on it.

2 A psychology teacher tells her students that they have failed on their first piece of coursework and asks them to write down what they think the reasons for this failure are. She is interested in whether they give internal or external justifications for the failure (e.g. 'I'm not very good at psychology' versus 'The teacher is useless'). She then explains that they have all passed.

3 You decide it would be interesting to see what strangers do if you sit next to them on the bus when there is plenty of space elsewhere.

4 You measure the effect of 3 units of alcohol on reaction time in sixth formers.

5 You observe how long people spend trying on clothes in a shop with communal changing rooms or closed cubicles.

Research on non-human animals

This will only be dealt with very briefly as, *before conducting experimental research on non-human animals, it is necessary for the premises, the researcher and the project to have a Home Office licence for that research.* Thus it is likely that any research on animals the readers of this book carry out will be non-experimental in nature – such as an observational study. Even here you should consider ethical issues. For example, you should not expose the animals to any more stress or disturbance than they usually meet.

If you are an A-level student any research on animals other than observational studies should be discussed beforehand with your lecturer, who might contact the exam board for advice.

Section Nine

- Summary tables
- Graphical representation
    Line graphs
    Histograms and bar charts
    Pie charts
    Stem and leaf diagrams
    Box and whisker plots
    Scattergrams and correlations
- Measures of central tendency
    Mean
    Median
    Mode
- Distribution curves
    Normal distributions
    Skewed distributions
    Bimodal distributions
- Measures of the spread of scores
    Range
    Semi-interquartile range
    Standard deviation and variance
- Standard scores and z-scores

Presentation of data in reports

This involves the use of **descriptive statistics**. Don't panic at the mention of the word statistics – you will probably find that you are already familiar with nearly all of the material in this section.

Descriptive statistics – as the name indicates – are simply ways of summarising your research findings that do not go beyond description. They enable you to present your data so that someone else can see at a glance what you found, rather than being presented with lists of raw scores.

Even though you are probably familiar with this material do read the next section – what you are asked about this in a psychology exam will not be the same as in a maths exam!

The eyeball test   Students often underestimate the importance and usefulness of just looking carefully at the raw data. Don't underestimate the importance of the eyeball test – plus a dollop of common sense! For instance are the means of two sets of scores very different from each other? If they are, yet when you work out more complex statistics these indicate that there is no difference between the sets of scores, then perhaps you have gone wrong somewhere!

Tables of scores

These provide the most basic way to present a summary of your data. *Always make sure they have an informative title and are clearly labelled.* (See example below.)

If your research hypothesis suggests that there may be a *difference* between the sets of scores, you should present at least one *measure of central tendency* and one *measure of dispersion*. (These are discussed fully later in this section.) For example:

Table 9.1 Summary table to show the number of trigrams recalled

	Immediate recall	After 15-second delay	After 30-second delay
Mean	6.7	5.1	4.2
Median	6.0	4.5	4.0
Range	4	6	6
Standard deviation	1.22	2.45	2.66

If your research hypothesis suggests that there will be a *correlation* between two variables, it may not be meaningful to give means or medians. A measure of the spread of the two sets of scores (such as the range or **standard deviation**) might still be useful, however.

If you have tested a fairly small number of participants in a correlational study, you could present the data in a table as shown below. If there is going to be a long list of scores, it is better to include them in an appendix.

Example

Table 9.2 Table to show stress scores (max. 100) and illness scores (max. 40)

	Stress score	Illness score
P1	62	14
P2	81	22
P3	44	8
P4	77	22
P5	64	11
P6	88	32
P7	80	30
P8	55	9
Range	88 − 44 = 44	32 − 8 = 24

Note: If you are using the correlational method, you must always draw a scatter-gram. (See p. 105 for an explanation.)

Graphical representation

It is good practice to draw some kind of pictorial representation of the results. Perhaps you are used to calling anything drawn on graph paper a 'graph', but there are, in fact, different types of 'graph' – each with their own uses.

Line graphs

These show a trend over time or as a participant's experiences change. For example, if you were investigating the effect of room temperature on word recall you might draw a graph like this:

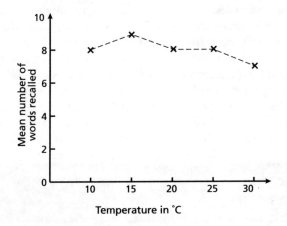

Figure 9.1 **Graph to show the effect of temperature on the mean number of words recalled by twenty participants**

Beware! For a line graph to be appropriate, the units of measurement along the bottom axis must be **continuous** not **discrete** data. On a *continuous* scale (such as length in metres or time in seconds) there is no limit to the subdivisions of the scale that can occur (e.g. 3.5 metres/3.57452 metres; 46.8 seconds/46.701 seconds). In theory, measurements can go to a minute fraction of a unit. With a *discrete* scale this is not the case – each point is separate from the next (e.g. number of children in a family or number of words recalled: it is not possible to have 2.13 children or to recall 5.67 words!).

A common mistake is to draw a graph like this:

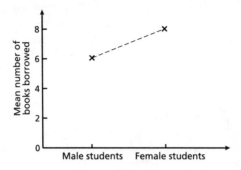

Figure 9.2 **Graph to show the mean number of books male and female students borrowed from a library in one term**

Does this mean that there are some hermaphrodites who borrow an average of seven books a term?

Another common error is to draw a line graph with *participants along the bottom axis*. These are often to be found in students' reports but are usually meaningless. They look impressive – especially if drawn by computer – but they mean nothing and get no marks. Why?

Compare these two graphs:

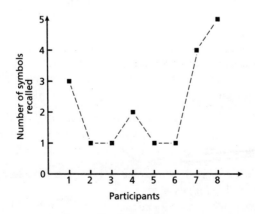

Figure 9.3 **Recall of Chinese symbols after a 30-second delay**

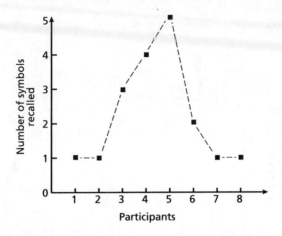

Figure 9.4 **Recall of Chinese symbols after a 30-second delay**

Although they look different, in fact the data represented on them is *exactly the same*. If the participants had been tested in a different order then the second graph would be produced rather than the first. The order of testing is due to chance – and thus the shape of the graph is due to chance as well. *So don't draw line graphs with 'participants' along the bottom axis!*

This might be a good place to add two warnings about computer-generated graphs:

• Make sure they are fully labelled.
• Don't get carried away with them. One useful graph is all that is needed. Fifteen – all showing basically the same thing – gain no more marks!

Histograms and bar charts

These are often confused or regarded as being the same thing. They do, in fact, have different uses.

Histograms can be drawn for *continuous data*. Cardwell, Clark and Meldrum (1996) define them as a 'type of frequency distribution where the number of scores in each category is represented by a vertical column'. The scale or classes are shown on the horizontal axis, with the frequency shown on the vertical axis. For example:

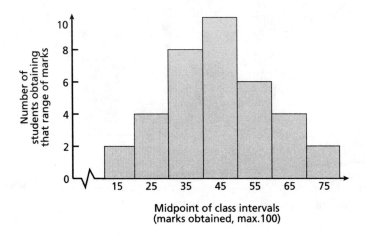

Figure 9.5 **Histogram of marks obtained in a mock psychology exam**

The horizontal axis above could be marked with the range of each interval thus:

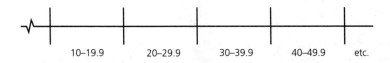

but this can be cumbersome and it is often easier to mark the mid-points.

The *bar chart* is used for *discrete data* such as the number of males or females, nationality, and so on.

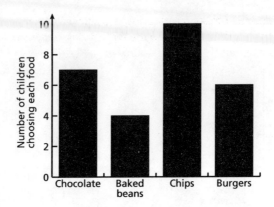

Figure 9.6 **Bar chart to show the favourite foods of six-year-olds**

The columns of a bar chart are usually separated.

Both histograms and bar charts are a type of frequency chart.

It can be useful to draw bar charts or histograms which show the data from two different groups of participants:

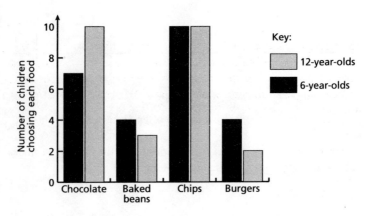

Figure 9.7 **Bar chart showing the favourite foods of six- and twelve-year-olds**

If you draw a histogram with a dot in the centre of the top of each column and join these up, you will have drawn a *frequency polygon*. Thus the histogram above could be drawn:

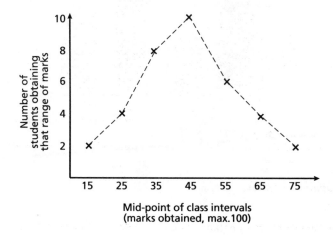

Figure 9.8 **Frequency of marks obtained in a mock psychology exam**

These consist of a circle divided into sections so that each section represents the proportion contributed to the whole. You cannot draw a pie chart unless you have all the relevant information. For instance, in the example below, you need to know the destination of all the students.

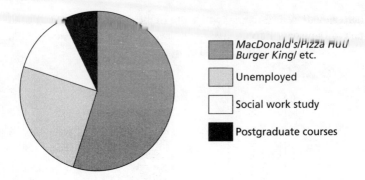

Figure 9.9 **Pie chart to show the destination of sociology students leaving university in 1997**

General points on drawing graphs

* *Beware of the 'Gee Whizz' graph.* This is a graph which looks dramatic – but only because of the scale used on each axis.

This can happen because part of an axis is omitted, as in a) below:

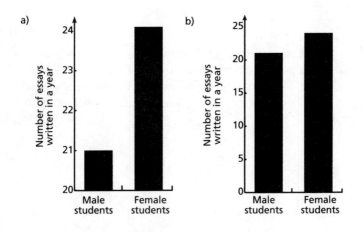

Figure 9.10 **A comparison of graphs**

There should be a break shown in the vertical axis of the first bar chart to show that the scale from 0 to 20 has been chopped off:

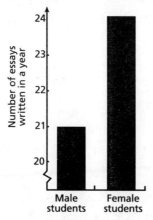

Figure 9.11 **A corrected 'Gee Whizz' graph**

Even then it is a very biased graph!

The 'Gee Whizz' effect can also occur when an inappropriate scale is used:

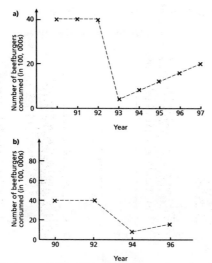

Figure 9.12 **Mean number of beefburgers eaten since 'mad cow' disease**

The graphs above use the same information but look very different.

- Be careful that you *label everything* really clearly. When you miss a label, you lose marks for your coursework!

Stem and leaf diagrams

These are useful for condensing large amounts of data, and often reveal patterns in the data.

Suppose you conduct an experiment to see how long participants take to solve anagrams of food-related words before and after a large meal. The results are as follows:

Before (time in seconds):	1.7	2.8	2.3	2.3	3.6	4.7	4.6	4.5
After (time in seconds):	3.3	3.3	3.4	3.5	4.5	4.7	4.9	5.2

If these scores were arranged as a **stem and leaf diagram** they would look like this:

Time taken to solve food-related anagrams

Before the meal				After the meal			
			7	1			
8	3	3		2			
			6	3	3	3	4	5
7	6	5		4	5	7	9
				5	2		

The numbers down the middle strip show the whole numbers; the numbers either side show the decimal points. Thus 5.2 is shown as:

| | 5 | 2 |

You can see that the stem and leaf diagram gives a good indication of the 'shape' of the data and, at the same time, all the scores are represented so that none of the data is lost.

Stem and leaf diagrams can be very useful – and they are quick and easy to produce.

Box and whisker plots

These are a useful indicator of the spread of scores. The 'box' represents the middle 50 per cent of the data, the 'whiskers' show the range and a cross shows the median.

For example, for the set of scores: 2 4 6 8 10 12 14, a box and whisker plot would look like this:

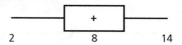

Figure 9.13 A box and whisker plot

Box and whisker plots can provide a useful indicator of any skew in the scores. Figure 9.13 shows a **normal distribution**, while Figures 9.14 and 9.15 indicate **skewed distributions**:

Figure 9.14 A positive skew

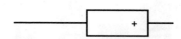

Figure 9.15 A negative skew

Exercise 30

What is wrong with the following table and figures? Each has at least two faults.

Table 9.3 Table of results		
	Group A	Group B
P1	4	7
P2	6	8
P3	4	6
P4	5	5
P5	3	7
P6	2	8
Mean	4	6.83
Median	4	7

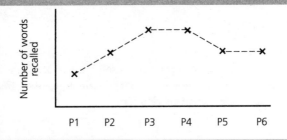

Figure 9.16

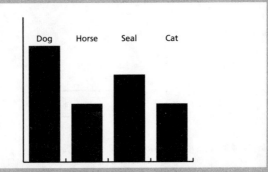

Figure 9.17 **Histogram to show favourite animals**

Scattergrams or scattergraphs

These are used to illustrate the findings of correlational research and indicate the pattern of the relationship between two variables. The easiest way to demonstrate their use is to give an example:

Table 9.4 Table to show shoe size at the age of nine and height at the age of eighteen

	Shoe size at 9	Height at 18
P1	1	6'2"
P2	10	5'10"
P3	11	5'11"
P4	1	6'0"
P5	10	5'11"
P6	2	6'2"
P7	8	5'8"
P8	9	5'10"
P9	11	6'0"
P10	12	6'1"

To plot this data on to a scattergram:

1   Label one axis with height and one with shoe size. (It doesn't really matter which is which.)

2   For P1 find their shoe size on the relevant axis and find their height on the other axis.

3   Work up from the horizontal axis and across from the vertical axis and place a cross where the lines meet.

4   Repeat for all the other scores.

For the data above you would have a scattergram which looks like this:

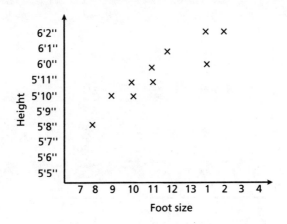

Figure 9.18 **Scattergram of height versus shoe size**

You can see that the crosses tend to go diagonally across the graph thus:

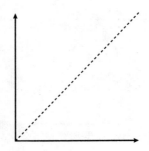

A tendency for the crosses to lie in this direction suggests a *positive correlation* – as the size of one variable increases the size of the other increases as well.

Another example would look quite different:

Table 9.5 Table to show rail fares and number of passengers	
Rail fare	*Number of passengers*
$20	250
$24	240
$28	220
$32	190
$36	190
$40	170

Plotted as a scattergram the data would look like this:

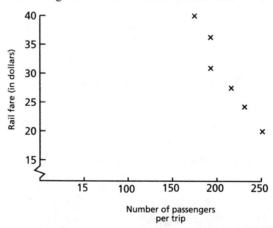

Figure 9.19 Scattergram of fares versus number of passengers

You can see that the crosses tend to go diagonally across the graph thus:

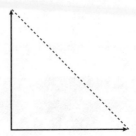

A tendency for the crosses to lie in this direction suggests a *negative correlation* – as one variable increases the other decreases.

If there is *no relationship* between the variables then a scattergram might look like this:

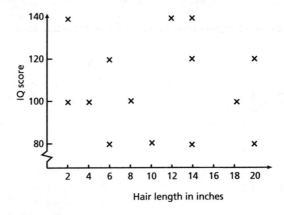

Figure 9.20 **Scattergram of hair length versus IQ score**

Think of two examples of your own when you would expect to find:

- a positive correlation
- a negative correlation
- no correlation

Sometimes a scattergram might show an inverted relationship like this:

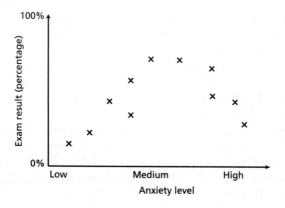

Figure 9.21 **Scattergram of anxiety levels versus exam results**

or this:

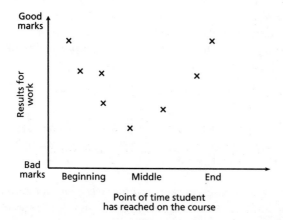

Figure 9.22 **Scattergram of the point of time a student has reached on a course versus their results**

Such a result demonstrates the importance of drawing a scattergram. As you can see there is a 'U-shaped' relationship between the variables.

In Figure 9.21 the variables initially increase together and then decrease together. You might obtain such a graph if you compared anxiety with exam performance, as the scattergram shows. Very low anxiety – perhaps because the student does not see the result as important – correlates with a low grade; some anxiety is helpful and correlates with a better grade; really high anxiety leads to panic and the grade gets lower again.

In Figure 9.22 the variables decrease together and then increase together, as might occur if you plotted the relationship between the length of time spent doing a course and results. On beginning the course, the student works hard – and their results are good; a few months into the course, the work rate tails off – and so do the results; towards the end of the course things seem more urgent again, so the work rate increases – and so do the grades obtained.

Both of these examples illustrate the importance of drawing a scattergram. There clearly is some kind of relationship between the variables involved *but this would not be shown by a statistical test of correlation such as Pearson's product moment or Spearman's rank order test.* Such tests are not sensitive to inverted relationships like those above and would just indicate there was a high probability that any relationship was due to chance.

Correlation coefficients

The relationship between two variables, as well as being described by scattergrams, can be expressed by a **correlation coefficient**. This is a mathematical way to show how closely related two variables are.

- If two variables have a *perfect positive correlation* – for example, if you measured foot size and height and found that *everyone* with Size 6 feet was 5'5", *everyone* with Size 7 feet was 5'6", and so on – the correlation coefficient would be +1.0.
- If two variables have a *perfect negative correlation* – for example, if you found that for each unit of alcohol consumed each week exam grades went down one mark – the correlation coefficient would be −1.0.

- If there is *no relationship* – for example, if you measure length of hair and exam grades – the correlation coefficient would be 0.

The closer a correlation is to +1.0, the greater the positive correlation between the variables. Thus, assuming sample size to be constant, a correlation of +0.8 shows a closer relationship between two sets of scores than one of +0.3.

Similarly, the closer a correlation is to −1.0, the greater the negative correlation between the variables. Given constant sample sizes, a correlation of −0.7 shows a closer relationship between two sets of scores than one of −0.5.

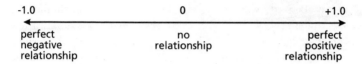

Plotted on a scattergram it would look like this:

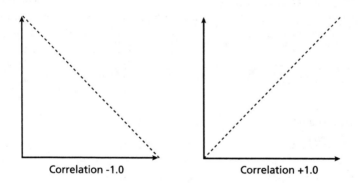

Variations might look something like this:

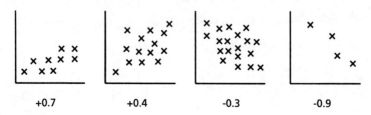

Don't confuse *no relationship* between variables and *a negative relationship*. A correlation of −0.8 is just as strong as one of +0.8.

Draw rough scattergrams to show what the following would look like:

1 a correlation of −0.6
2 a correlation of +1.0
3 a correlation of +0.2
4 a correlation of −0.9
5 a correlation of 0.0

Measures of central tendency

These are ways of estimating the mid-point of a set of scores. They are often referred to as **averages** and you are probably familiar with all of them.

There are three different measures of **central tendency**:

• the **mean**
• the **median**
• the **mode**

The mean

This is the arithmetic average of the scores. To calculate it you add up all the numbers in the set of scores and divide by the number of scores that there are.

Advantages of the mean   The mean has the advantage that it is very sensitive. It extracts the most information from the scores, because all the raw data is used in its calculation. For this reason it is commonly used for data at the interval **level of measurement** (see

Section Ten). As long as the scores are not in a *skewed* or **bimodal distribution** it is very useful. (See the part of this section on distribution curves for further details.)

Disadvantages of the mean Disadvantages arise, however, precisely because of this sensitivity. If scores are very widespread, or cluster around two values, the mean can be misleading. For example, if you had to organise a children's party and were told that the mean age of the children was eight years of age, what games would you plan? Whatever you have just decided might be okay if the children's ages were 6, 7, 8, 8, 8, 8, 9 and 10, but suppose that the ages were 1, 2, 3, 8, 13, 14 and 15 or 4, 4, 4, 4, 12, 12, 12 and 12 – the mean of all these lists is 8!

> The above example shows why it is a good idea to give a measure of spread, as well as the mid-point, when you summarise scores.

Example

A disadvantage of the mean is that it can be greatly affected by extreme scores. I once taught a student who did a piece of coursework on the effect of being watched when doing a simple jigsaw puzzle. She tested nine participants who took between 16 and 25 seconds to complete the jigsaw. The tenth participant was her eighty-nine-year-old grandfather who took 126 seconds. This score had a dramatic effect on the mean. The median was 19 seconds but the mean was 30.6 seconds!

The median

This is the central number in a set of scores. To calculate it you arrange the scores in order and find the mid-point. If there are an odd number of scores the median will be the central number. For example in this list:

2, 3, 6, 8, 9, 10, 11, 13 and 13

the median would be 9.

If there are an even number of scores the median will be halfway between the middle two scores. For example in this list:

2, 2, 5, 6, 8, 9, 9 and 10

the median will be 7.

Advantages of the median   The advantage of the median is that it is not affected by an extreme score. If the last score in the above list was 30 rather than 10, the median would still be 7.

Disadvantages of the median   The disadvantage of the median is that it is not as sensitive as the mean, because not all the raw scores are used in its calculation.

The mode

This is simply the most common score in a list. For example in this list:

2, 3, 4, 4, 4, 5, 6 and 6

the mode would be 4.

There can be two (or more) modes. The distribution is then said to be *bimodal* if there are two modes, and **multimodal** if there are more than two. For example in this list:

2, 2, 2, 4, 6, 6, 6, 7 and 8

there are two modes – 2 and 6.

Advantages of the mode   The mode is useful when knowledge about the frequency of an event is important, or when data is discrete.

Examples

- If you are the buyer for a dress shop where 40 per cent of the customers are Size 12, 20 per cent are Size 14 and 40 per cent are Size 16, it does not make sense to buy lots of Size 14 dresses just because this size is the mean and median.
- For discrete data, such as the number of children in a family, it is better to say that the modal figure for the British family is 2 rather than to say that the mean is 2.334!

Disadvantages of the mode A disadvantage is that the mode is rarely useful in small sets of data when there are often several modes.

If there is a large difference between the mean, the median and the mode, this indicates a *skewed distribution* or possibly a *bimodal distribution*. If all three are similar this indicates a *normal distribution*.

1 List one advantage and one disadvantage for:

- the mean
- the median
- the mode

2 Calculate the mean, median and mode for the following sets of scores:

   (a) 2, 2, 3, 5, 6, 6, 6, 9, 13, 15 and 21
   (b) 4, 4, 5, 5, 6, 6, 7, 7, 7, 8 and 8
   (c) 2, 3, 7, 8, 9, 9, 10, 11, 12, 12, 12 and 12

Exercise 33a

Distribution curves

Normal distributions

If researchers make a very large number of observations of human characteristics they often find that many physical and psychological variables are distributed in the total population in a pattern known as a *normal distribution*. If this data is presented on a graph or frequency curve, it has a symmetrical, somewhat bell-like shape. This is known as a *normal curve*.

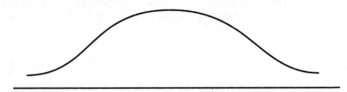

Figure 9.23 **A normal distribution curve**

Example

Suppose we measured the height of all the females studying psychology at one college and represented the data as a histogram. It might look like this:

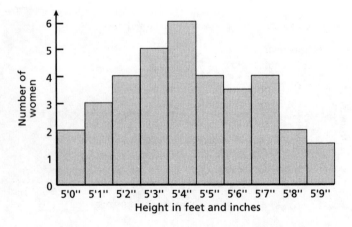

Figure 9.24 **Histogram to show the height of female students at Blogsville College**

A frequency distribution curve of these results would look like this:

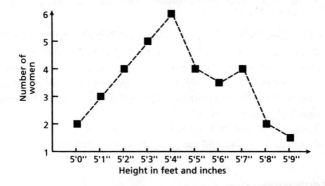

Figure 9.25 **Frequency distribution curve of the height of female students at Blogsville College**

(For this sample there are more scores in the 'middle' than at the 'ends' but there is not a normal distribution.)

However, if we expanded our sample to every female studying psychology in England, we should find that the result approximates to a normal curve and looks like this:

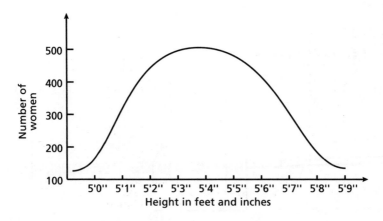

Figure 9.26 **Frequency distribution curve of the height of all female psychology students in England**

For this much larger sample we probably would obtain something very close to a normal distribution curve.

All normal distribution curves share four characteristics:

- They are symmetrical about the mean.
- The ends of the curve never reach zero: i.e. they never reach the horizontal axis. (Actually they reach it at infinity – but even statisticians don't know where that is!)
- They are roughly bell-shaped.
- The mean, median and mode are all at the same point.

Skewed distributions

Sometimes, when a frequency distribution curve is plotted, the distribution is lop-sided, or *skewed*. The skew may be *positive*:

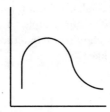

Figure 9.27 **A positive skew**

or negative:

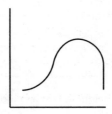

Figure 9.28 **A negative skew**

Having spent many years completely unable to remember which was which, I was shown the following mnemonic:

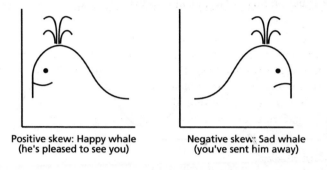

Positive skew: Happy whale   Negative skew: Sad whale
(he's pleased to see you)   (you've sent him away)

Figure 9.29 **Happy and sad wales**

It is characteristic of a skewed distribution that the mean, median and mode will have different values (whereas in a normal distribution they will be the same). The *mean* will be towards the tail because it is swayed by extreme scores. The *mode* will be the highest point. The *median* will be between the two.

You often obtain a skewed distribution if:

- You have a biased sample.
- You only test a small sample.
- There are **floor** or **ceiling effects**.

Floor and ceiling effects might occur if the measurement instrument that you are using in your research fails to discriminate adequately between your participants. For example, if you were testing IQ scores and you gave your participants a test which was too hard for them, they might all obtain 0, 1 or 2 out of 30. This would be a *floor effect*. If, on the other hand, you gave them a test which was much too easy, they might all obtain 28, 29 or 30 out of 30. This would be a *ceiling effect*.

A floor effect will produce a positive skew and a ceiling effect will produce a negative skew.

Bimodal distributions

Sometimes that data collected has two modes, and this results in a distribution curve which might look like this:

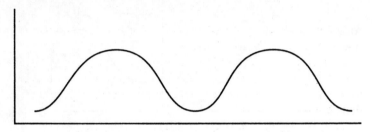

Figure 9.30 **A bimodal distribution**

This is known as a *bimodal distribution curve*.

Exercise 33b

Look back at your answers for Exercise 33a, Question 2.

1   What type of distribution is shown by each of the above lists?
2   If the mean, median and mode were as follows, what would be the rough shape of the distribution of scores?

(a) Mean 8.3, median 8 and modes 9 and 7
(b) Mean 8.9, median 9 and mode 9.

Measures of dispersion or variability

If measures of central tendency are a measure of the 'middleness' of a set of scores, then measures of **dispersion** or variability are a measure of their 'spread-outness'. When summarising a set of scores you should always include an indication of their *spread*, as well as their mid-point.

Consider the following sets of scores:

10	20	30	40	50	60	70	80	90	Mean = 50; median = 50
35	40	45	50	50	50	55	60	65	Mean = 50; median = 50

Although the means and medians are identical for the two lists, the spread of the scores is very different.

Knowledge of this could be very important. For example it could indicate greater participant variability in the first list – if the scores were test results there would be a much greater spread of ability in the first group of students.

The most common measures of dispersion are:

- the **range**
- the **semi-interquartile range**
- the **standard deviation**

The range

The range is a crude measure of the spread of a set of scores, calculated by subtracting the lowest of value from the highest value. In the sets of scores above:

- the range of the first set would be $90 - 10 = 80$
- the range of the second would be $65 - 35 = 30$

Measurement error can easily occur. Imagine you are measuring how many seconds it takes someone to complete a simple jigsaw. If you time them at 57 seconds, the watch could have just moved to 57 (more accurately their time might have been 57.02) or it could be about to move to 58 (more accurately 57.97).

This raises an interesting issue. It is common practice for *statisticians* to state the following: add 1 to allow for measurement error if the unit of measurement is whole units (5, 8, etc.); if you are measuring in units to one decimal place (1.3, 2.8, etc.), then add 0.1; if you are measuring in units to two decimal places (1.67, 3.97, etc.), add 0.01, and so on. The reason I say this is interesting is because every *mathematician* I have spoken to says that the range is such a crude measure anyway it isn't worth doing this. I can see the logic in both arguments – but for the sake of simplicity I think I side with the mathematicians!

The *advantages* of the range are that it is easy to calculate and that it shows the extreme values. The *disadvantages* are that it is distorted by extreme scores and that it gives no information as to whether scores are clustered around the mean or are evenly spread out. For example, the ranges of 1 7 7 8 9 9 17 and 1 3 5 7 9 11 13 15 17 are exactly the same.

The semi-interquartile range

This shows the range of the middle 50 per cent of a set of scores.

A 'quartile' is 25 per cent of the scores.

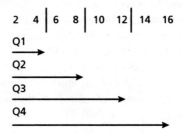

The semi-interquartile range is the range of the middle two quartiles, i.e. (from the example above) $12 - 6$, which equals 6.

The *advantage* of the semi-interquartile range is that it is not affected by extreme scores. (You are not expected to calculate it in A-level psychology, but you may meet it in some computer programs.)

Variance

This is a measure of the average spread of a set of scores around the mean. In other words it shows the variation among the scores. It is widely used in statistical tests but not as widely quoted as a stand-alone measure as its close relative, the standard deviation.

The standard deviation (SD)

This is a measure of the average spread of scores around the mean. It is the square root of the **variance**, and a much more sensitive descriptor of the dispersion of scores than is the range. When calculating the range and the semi-interquartile range only a few scores are taken into account, but with the standard deviation (and variance too) every score is used.

If a set of scores has a large standard deviation or wide variance, this indicates a wide distribution of scores. If a set of scores has a small standard deviation or narrow variance, then this indicates a narrow distribution of scores.

The calculation for both the variance and the standard deviation involves working out the difference between each individual score and the mean for the sample. These differences are then squared (thus getting rid of any differences in sign), added together and divided by the total number of scores (to calculate the variance for the sample) or by $n - 1$ (to calculate the variance for the total population). The standard deviation is the square root of this number.

The formula for calculating standard deviation (SD) for a sample of scores is:

$$\sqrt{\frac{\sum (x - \bar{x})^2}{n}}$$

where

n = the number of scores in the set
x = an individual score
$\bar{x}$ = the mean of the sample

The formula for calculating the SD when, as is the usual case, we are interested in the standard deviation of the sample as an estimate of the SD of the population is:

$$\sqrt{\frac{\sum (x - \bar{x})^2}{n - 1}}$$

In fact, calculating the standard deviation by hand is a tedious process and it is more usual nowadays to use a scientific calculator. It will tell you what to do in the instruction book. Alternatively you may have access to a computer program or spreadsheet which will work out standard deviation for you.

If you have data at the ordinal level or if there is an obvious skew to the distribution of the scores then it may be inappropriate to calculate the standard deviation, as it is based on the assumptions that the data is suitable for arithmetic calculations and that there is a normal distribution of scores in the total population.

What does a standard deviation score tell you?

Even if you do not calculate the standard deviation in your own coursework, you should be sure that you understand how to interpret it.

When you calculate standard deviation you get a number – something like 1.58 or 3.49. What does this mean? There are really only two points you need to understand:

- The larger the SD the greater the spread of scores.
- The SD can be used to interpret how usual or unusual any individual's particular score is.

Example: Standard deviation as an indicator of the spread of a set of scores

- A class obtains scores of 45, 46, 47, 48, 49 and 50 on a test with a maximum score of 75.

Here the scores are not widely spread and look roughly like this on a 'dotplot'.

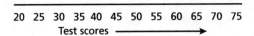

The standard deviation for this sample is small. It is 1.71.

- If the scores were 20, 45, 46, 47, 48, 49, 50 and 75 the spread would look very different.

```
        .           . . . . . .                    .
   20  25  30  35  40  45  50  55  60  65  70  75
              Test scores  ──────────▶
```

For this sample the standard deviation is 13.83.

```
   . .       . .                    . .          . .
   20  25  30  35  40  45  50  55  60  65  70  75
              Test scores  ──────────▶
```

- For the set of scores 20 21 30 31 60 61 74 and 75 the spread of scores is different again.

The standard deviation is 23.38.

You can see that the size of the standard deviation differs according to the 'spread-outness' of the scores.

For the last two examples you can see that the *range* would be exactly the same. However, the greater sensitivity of the standard deviation – due to the fact that all the scores are used in its calculation – indicates that the 'spread-outness' of the set of scores is different.

Standard deviation as an aid to the interpretation of single scores

The standard deviation is also used in the interpretation of individual scores. This interpretation is based on the relationship that exists between the standard deviation and the normal distribution curve.

In the section on the normal curve (see p. 116), it states that a normal distribution curve is symmetrical about the mean. If drawn it would look like this:

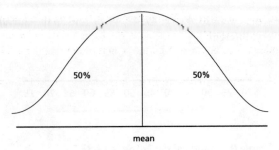

Figure 9.31 **A normal distribution curve plus the mean**

Thus half the scores are above the mean and half are below it. In other words if you compare the score of any individual with the mean, it tells you whether that person is in the top 50 per cent or the bottom 50 per cent of the sample.

This is very obvious, and applying standard deviation to the normal curve is just an extension of this. As it is true that there is a constant relationship between the mean and the normal distribution, this is also true for the standard deviation. If the value of one standard deviation is marked above or below the mean in *any* normal distribution, approximately 34 per cent of the population will fall between the mean and one standard deviation above or below the mean. The following example shows a normal distribution curve of a large centre's exam marks. The mean mark is 50 out of 100 and the standard deviation is 5. You can see that the mean and one SD above and below the mean are marked on the curve.

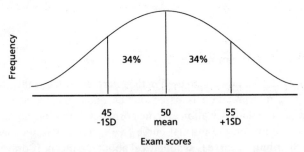

Figure 9.32 **A normal distribution curve marked with the mean and +1 and −1 standard deviation**

Approximately 34 per cent of the students will have scored between 50 and 55 and approximately 34 per cent will have scored between 45 and 50. (If you want to be more precise the actual percentage is 34.13 per cent.)

If a further standard deviation is marked on either side thus:

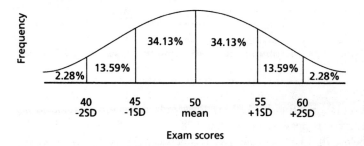

Figure 9.33 **A normal distribution curve marked with the mean and +2 and −2 standard deviations**

then a further 13.59 per cent will fall in this band and the remaining 2.28 per cent will fall above the +2SD or below the −2SD mark.

Don't panic at this point! All will become clear with an example. You do not need to know how these numbers were calculated ... just how they can be used.

Example

Suppose 2,235 men were tested on an IQ test and the results obtained were:

mean = 100   standard deviation = 15

Shown on a graph this would look like this:

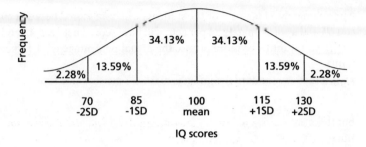

Figure 9.34 **Distribution curve showing the IQ scores of 2,235 men**

From the relationship between the standard deviation and the normal curve it is possible to see that 2.28 per cent of the group have IQs below 70, 13.59 per cent have IQs between 70 and 85, 34.13 per cent have IQs between 85 and 100 and so on. You can see that standard deviation allows us to interpret an individual's score in more depth. If Joe Bloggs scores 134, we can see that he is in the top 2.28 per cent. If Bert Smith scores 95, we can see that he falls in the 34.13 per cent just below the mean.

Exercise 34

1　What percentage have IQs between 100 and 130?
2　What percentage have IQs over 130?
3　What percentage have IQs between 85 and 115?
4　If individuals gained the scores 65, 110, 120 and 144, how would you interpret them in terms of where they fall in the overall distribution?

This relationship between the normal curve and standard deviation exists whatever the shape of the normal curve. Normal distribution curves do vary in shape:

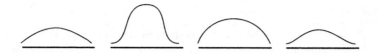

Figure 9.35 **Normal distribution curves**

but this relationship between the standard deviation and the distribution of the scores is always the same:

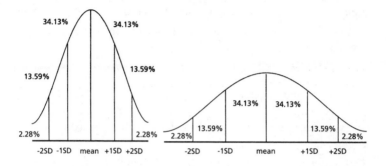

Figure 9.36 **Relationship between the standard deviation and the distribution of scores on different shaped distributions**

In a sample of 2,000 new-born babies, the mean birth weight was 3 kg and the standard deviation was 0.5 kg.

Draw a normal curve and mark on it the mean and two standard deviations above and below the mean.

1 What percentage of babies weighed under 2.5 kg?
2 What percentage weighed between 3.5 and 4 kg?
3 What percentage weighed under 2 kg?
4 What percentage weighed between 2.5 and 3.5 kg?

Exercise 35

Standard scores and z-scores

If a score is one standard deviation above the mean it is said to have a **standard score** or **z-score** of plus one $(+1)$. If a score is one standard deviation below the mean it has a standard score or a z-score of minus one (-1).

For instance, in the previous example of IQ test scores, 115 would have a standard score or z-score of $+1$ and 85 a standard score or z-score of -1. A score of 107.5 would be half a standard deviation above the mean and so would have a standard score or z-score of $+0.5$.

A standard score or z-score is calculated from the following formula:

$$z = \frac{\text{individual score} - \text{the mean}}{\text{standard deviation}}$$

For example, if Kate scores 130 on the IQ test, the standard score or z-score would be:

$$z = \frac{130 - 100}{15} = 2$$

Standard scores or z-scores are useful because you can use them to compare an individual's score across different tests, even though the marking scheme, the means and the standard deviations are very different for the various tests.

1 In a mock exam two groups of psychology students obtain the following scores:

Group A	35	45	52	54	55	55	56	58	60	62	64	68	73
Group B	30	33	37	38	43	44	45	50	52	55	55	57	75

   (a) What is the range of each set of scores?
   (b) What is the limitation of using the range as a measure of distribution in this example?

2 What is meant by standard deviation?
3 Draw a rough sketch of a normal distribution of scores with a mean of 40 and a standard deviation of 4. What percentage of people score above 48? below 36? between 32 and 40?
4 A researcher measures the time it takes 100 students to read a 960-word article on statistics. The results are normally distributed and have a mean of 25 minutes and a standard deviation of 5 minutes. They then measure the time it takes the same students to read a 960-word article entitled 'Ten ways to keep your lover happy'. The results have a positive skew with a mean of 9 minutes and a median of 7 minutes.

   (a) Draw the distribution curve for the two examples.
   (b) What percentage of students take the following times to read the statistics article: over 30 minutes? between 30 and 35 minutes? under 25 minutes?

Exercise 36

Section Ten

- Explanation of the different levels of measurement

Measurement

As has already been explained, research data can be divided into two types: qualitative and quantitative. In any quantitative research, numbers will be assigned to variables – but numbers can carry differing amounts of information. Assigning numbers may involve:

- simply *counting* (e.g. how many participants fall into a certain category), or
- *measuring* a variable (e.g. how many seconds people take to complete a task)

In other words *numbers can represent different levels of detail in different circumstances*. This difference in the levels of information that can be carried by numbers is referred to as different *levels of measurement*.

The levels of measurement that can be used are:

- **nominal**
- **ordinal**
- **interval**
- **ratio**

> The mnemonic *N O I R* may help you remember this:
> *N*ominal/*O*rdinal/*I*nterval/*R*atio

Data at the nominal level

Data at the nominal level is the simplest. The data collected is placed in *categories* and you just *count* how many participants fall into each category. For example, you could count how many participants are male or female; have passed or not passed their driving test; are aged under 20/21–40/41–60/over 60.

If you are collecting data at the nominal level you will probably use tallies as you collect it. For example:

Stopped at zebra crossing	IIII IIII II
Failed to stop	IIII IIII IIII III

Here each observation is being placed in a *category* and *frequencies* are being counted. Data at the nominal level provides the least amount of information of all the levels. For instance, I might say that the temperature today is above freezing or below freezing. This would give you some information about the weather – but not a lot.

Data at the ordinal level

Data at the ordinal level (as the name implies!) puts things in order. In an ordinal scale, each number represents a position in the group – such as first, second, third, etc. in an exam.

If I used an ordinal scale for weather, I might rate the temperature on the following scale:

Very cold	Cold	Slightly cold	Slightly hot	Hot	Very hot

This obviously provides more detail than data at the nominal level – but you still don't have the full picture. After all, what I think is 'very hot' might just be 'hot' to you.

Data at the ordinal level can be used to put results in order (or **ranks** to use the statistical jargon) but *it gives no information about the size of the interval between the positions.* If you ask tourists to rate the hotels they have stayed at as 'very good', 'good', 'medium', 'poor' or 'very poor', this would enable you to put the hotels into a rank order. However, it does not imply that there are equal intervals between the categories. You know that 'good' is better than 'poor' – but is the gap between 'very good' and 'good' the same size as the gap between 'poor' and 'very poor'?

Data at the interval level

Data at the interval level is measured on a scale which has precise and equal intervals. Temperature is a good example. If I tell you that the temperature today is 24°C, you can judge more accurately what the weather was like. Data at the interval level carries much more information than ordinal data.

Data at the ratio level

Data at the ratio level has all the characteristics of interval data, plus it has a true zero point. For example weight in grams is a ratio scale, as something cannot weigh -6 g. *All ratio scales are interval scales as well.*

Interval and ratio data are sometimes both referred to as *cardinal scales.*

Summary so far…
Nominal level Data counted in categories (yes/no)
Ordinal level Puts the results into an order (first/second/third)
Interval level Data measured on a precise scale (°C)
Ratio level Like the interval level, but no negative values (seconds)

Why is knowledge of levels of measurement important?

Only data measured on interval or ratio scales is on a true *quantitative scale*. This means that it is acceptable to carry out arithmetic operations on the actual numerical values collected:

- As the calculation of the *mean* involves arithmetic calculations, purists argue that the mean should only be calculated when you have interval data. (Its use on ordinal data does seem to be widely accepted, but this doesn't mean that it's correct!)
- **Parametric tests** assume that the scores obtained have been measured on an interval or ratio scale. It is not valid to use parametric tests on data at the ordinal level. (There is more discussion in Section 11, which deals with test selection.)

You need to be able to recognise whether a measurement scale is nominal, ordinal or interval/ratio before you can decide which is the most appropriate statistical test to use.

Having said this I must warn you that trying to get agreement amongst psychologists as to what is and what is not interval data, is harder than trying to get two Chief Examiners to agree as to whose A-level syllabus is the better. If you go to some universities to study psychology, they will take a very hard line and teach you that *no* measurements of human characteristics ever reach a true interval scale. They may argue for example that, even with times taken to run an Olympic heat, measurement in seconds may *appear* to represent interval/ratio data, but in fact – because it is harder and harder to run faster and faster – the times do not accurately represent the difficulty of achieving these speeds. Other universities may take a far more lenient line and treat almost anything that involves collecting numbers as interval-level data.

How is the poor student supposed to sort this out? I suggest the following 'rules of thumb':

- If the measurements include attitudes or opinions or ratings, treat them as ordinal.
- Ask yourself if the difficulty involved in moving up the scale of equivalent intervals really involves the same effort or difficulty. For example, in a test of memory, is it as hard to improve your score

from three to six words, as it is to improve from seven to ten words? If you decide the answer is no, then treat the data as ordinal.

The real problem arises over measures (such as intelligence tests) where it is the aim of the psychometrist to devise a scale which *does* measure human ability at the interval level and as a result of a test that has been standardised. Some researchers argue that in an IQ test, measurement is at the ordinal level because some questions are harder than others, and it is possible that you and I both score 120 but don't get the same questions right. Thus are our scores really the same? On the other hand the psychometrists might argue that, through the procedures they use when formulating such tests, the results approach so closely to the interval level of measurement that they can be treated as such.

So what does the student conclude? Well – pragmatically speaking, in coursework or in an exam, either answer will have to be treated as correct. If you really want to decide which is the correct answer, as you might if you go on to conduct research of your own at postgraduate level, this is an issue that you will really have to determine for yourself – just as, to go back to my earlier analogy, a teacher has to come to their own decision as to which is the best exam syllabus for their students.

1   What level of measurement are the following?

  (a) The time taken to read an essay.
  (b) The number of males and females in your psychology class.
  (c) How hot it is today.
  (d) How much people say they like *Friends*.
  (e) How many people voted Labour or Conservative.
  (f) How highly people rate Tony Blair as Prime Minister.

2   Think of ways to measure driving skills that use data at the

  (a) nominal level
  (b) ordinal level
  (c) interval level

Exercise 37

Section Eleven

- Introduction to inferential statistics
- The use of parametric and non-parametric tests
- The selection of statistical tests

Check the syllabus that you are following to see whether knowledge of both *parametric and non-parametric tests is required.*

Tests of statistical inference

In Section Nine there are details of descriptive statistics such as the mean, median, range, and so on. As the name of such statistics implies, these only *describe* data. They do not enable you to draw any firm conclusions as to the likelihood that your results are due to chance, or whether the chance element is sufficiently low to enable you to reject your null hypothesis. To be able to draw these kind of conclusions, you need to use what you probably think of as 'proper' statistics (you may use a less polite word) – things with strange names like Spearman's rho and chi-square.

Why are you asked to carry out these tests in psychology?

The reason is that, when you test a hypothesis, you are likely to find that some of the data supports your research hypothesis but some of it does not. For example a psychologist might find that seventeen out of twenty people solve anagrams of food-related words faster when they are hungry. However, three out of twenty solve them faster when they have just eaten! Similar tests are used in biology and geography. For example a biologist might find that there is less moss growing on trees by the M6 than on trees alongside a country lane. But there is still some moss there! Thus the question arises as to whether there really is a difference between the two cases or whether the differences are just chance occurrences.

The purpose of using inferential statistical tests is to indicate how likely it is that the result that you have obtained in your study is due to chance.

All tests of statistical inference work in the same way:

- You choose the correct test.
- You do some (fairly) straightforward calculations – or use a computer program to do the calculations for you.
- At the end of the calculation you obtain an observed value (also called a calculated value) for that test.
- You compare this value with the critical value given in the appropriate table and this indicates the probability that your result was due to chance.

These steps will be explained in more detail in the following pages.

Different types of statistical tests

Inferential statistical tests can be divided into two types:

- parametric tests
- non-parametric tests

Parametric tests are called this because they make certain assumptions about the *parameters* of the population from which the sample has been drawn. For example they make assumptions about the spread of scores in the samples and the distribution of scores in the populations tested. In Section Twelve you will find details of how to calculate the following parametric tests: two types of *t*-tests and the Pearson product moment correlation coefficient.

> The eagle-eyed will have noticed that I have not mentioned the chi-square test here. It can be argued that this is a parametric test (see MacRae 1994), but it is commonly stated to be a non-parametric test by statistical textbooks! As it is designed for data measured on a nominal scale, the requirements that should be met before using the other parametric tests mentioned do not apply to chi-square.

Non-parametric tests (also called **distribution-free tests**) do not specify any assumptions about the nature of the population from which the scores have been collected. In Section Twelve there are details of how to calculate the following non-parametric tests: binomial sign test, Wilcoxon matched pairs, Mann–Whitney U-test and Spearman's rank order correlation coefficient.

When do you use a parametric or non-parametric test?

The selection of a statistical test is governed by certain rules – but there is also some controversy over whether parametric tests are actually suitable for use in behavioural sciences such as psychology (and, as you can see from the above, over what constitutes a parametric test!)

Parametric tests

Parametric tests are often preferred to non-parametric tests because they are more **powerful** and **robust**. What is meant by 'powerful' and 'robust'?

The *power* of a test refers to the likelihood that the test will detect a difference or a correlation between the sets of scores that have been collected. Parametric tests are more powerful because:

- Raw scores are used when calculating parametric tests. This means they are more sensitive as there is more information available than in a non-parametric test, which only uses ranked data. Parametric tests look at the size of values, not just the order.
- In general, parametric tests can be used on a smaller sample than non-parametric tests.

Tests are referred to as *robust* if errors do not occur in the results even though the assumptions underlying them are not fully met. It is argued by many statisticians (although not all) that parametric tests do not produce many errors if there are small violations of the underlying conditions.

However, the most powerful method is not always the most appropriate one to use. Formula One racing cars are much more powerful than ordinary cars but you wouldn't drive one to work. They are designed for use in certain conditions and are not appropriate for use under other conditions. Exactly the same is true of parametric tests. They too are designed for use under certain conditions, and in their case these conditions are:

Condition One: Data must be of interval or ratio level of measurement

As parametric tests involve sophisticated arithmetic operations, they are only suitable for data using the more precise interval or ratio levels of measurement.

Condition Two: Scores must be drawn from a normally distributed population

It is a basic assumption behind the logic of parametric tests that the characteristic being measured has a normal distribution in the total population. In a small-scale experiment you are unlikely to be able to check whether this is the case, and you can only check if the scores that you yourself have collected have a roughly normal distribution.

- You can plot the results graphically:

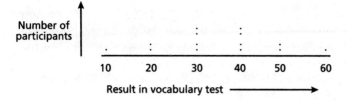

A result like this would show a normal distribution.

• Or you can compare the mean, median and mode. If the distribution is normal then these will all be similar.

Remember that the condition that has to be met is normal distribution *in the population*, not in the sample. However, if you have a marked skew in the sample this could possibly indicate a skewed distribution in the population. It is frequently argued that parametric tests are robust to small violations so a small skew can be ignored. However, don't use a parametric test if there is a marked skew.

Condition Three: Variability between sets of scores that have been collected must be similar

The variability of a set of scores can be measured in various ways:

• the range
• the standard deviation
• the variance (the square of the standard deviation)

Before running a parametric test you should check that there is not wide variability by calculating the standard deviation and the variance.

If you are in search of practical advice, Monk (1991) suggests the following guide to when it is unsafe to use a parametric test:

- If there are extreme scores – such as a score more than three standard deviations away from the mean.
- If the range of scores in one group is more than twice as large as in the other group.
- If there are ceiling or floor effects (i.e. if a test is so easy almost everyone has got nearly the highest possible score, or if it is so difficult that they have nearly all got low scores).

Summary

Before using a parametric test three criteria need to be met:

- *S*imilar variance in the two sets of scores
- *I*nterval or ratio measurement scales have been used
- *N*ormal distribution of scores in the population

(The mnemonic *SIN* might help you remember them.)

If these conditions are met, parametric tests give a more accurate estimate of the probability that the result is due to chance and so are usually used in preference to non-parametric tests.

Non-parametric tests

It is argued by some psychologists that, as the 'power efficiency' of non-parametric tests is *nearly* as high as that of parametric tests, it is a reasonable strategy always to use the former – especially as they are simpler to calculate. It is also argued that in a subject like psychology it is extremely difficult to be sure that the conditions for using parametric tests are ever fully met. Over forty years ago Siegel wrote:

as behavioural scientists rarely achieve the sort of measurement which permits the meaningful use of parametric tests, non-parametric statistical tests deserve an increasingly prominent role in research in the behavioural sciences.

(Siegel 1956: 31)

The decision as to whether a parametric or a non-parametric test is most appropriate is often contentious and this is a complex area for the student to understand. As has already been explained, the power of non-parametric tests is not much less than that of their parametric relations, and so their use is quite acceptable.

You should check the requirements of the course that you are following to make sure you have knowledge of the specified tests.

Comparison of parametric and non-parametric tests

Parametric	Non-parametric
More powerful	Less powerful – but the difference is not great
More sensitive	May need more participants to reach the same power as parametric equivalents
Robust, so can still be used even if the conditions for use are not *fully* met	Simpler to calculate

Test selection

This next section will cover the selection of statistical tests which are

- Testing for a difference between scores
- Testing for correlation

Before you can be confident that you are selecting an appropriate test you must be sure you understand *levels of measurement* and *experimental designs*. If you are a little hazy about these concepts revise them (Sections Three and Ten) before beginning this section.

Tests for a difference between two sets of scores

Data at the nominal level of measurement

- If you have data at the nominal level and an independent subject's design you can use the chi-square test.
- If you have data at the nominal level and a repeated measures design you can use the binomial sign test.

Data at the ordinal level of measurement

This also applies at the interval level when you don't have similar variance in the sets of scores collected or a probable normal distribution of scores in the total population (i.e. you don't have SIN).

- If you have data at the ordinal level (or interval level but not *SIN*) and an independent participants design you can use the Mann–Whitney U-test.
- If you have data at the ordinal level (or interval level but not *SIN*) and a repeated measures design you can use the Wilcoxon matched pairs test.

Data at the interval or ratio level

Plus similar variance in the sets of scores collected and a probable normal distribution of scores in the population.

- If you have data at the interval or ratio level (plus the other conditions for parametric tests) and an independent groups design you can use the *t*-test for independent data.
- If you have data at the interval or ratio level (plus the other conditions for parametic tests) and a repeated measures design you can use the *t*-test for related samples.

Robin Whale suggested the following mnemonic to me:

A*RE* YO*U* A *W*OMAN OR A *MAN* OR *BI*SEXUAL?

Organise the letters in italics thus:

R	*U*
W	*MAN*
BI	*X*

Add the test names and you have:

*R*elated *t*-test	*t*-test for *U*nrelated data
*W*ilcoxon matched pairs test	*MAN*n–Whitney U-test
*BI*nomial sign test	X^2 (chi-square test)

This fits them neatly into this table:

Tests for repeated measures	Tests for independent groups	
related *t*-test	*t*-test for unrelated data	*interval data + SIN*
Wilcoxon matched pairs test	Mann–Whitney U-test	*ordinal data*
binomial sign test	chi-square test (χ^2)	*nominal data*
Note: The parametric tests are on the upper line.		

Tests for correlation

When you have data at the *ordinal level of measurement* (or at the *interval level but not with similar variance or a normal distribution in the population*),

- you can use the Spearman's rank order correlation coefficient (Spearman's rho).

When you have data at the *interval* or *ratio levels of measurement* (*plus similar variance and a normal distribution in the population*),

- you can use the Pearson product moment correlation coefficient.

The tests for correlation can be tabulated as follows:

Ordinal level data	Interval level data
Spearman's rho	Pearson's product moment

Summary

Before you can decide on an appropriate test you must be able to answer the following questions:

- Are you testing to see if there is a difference or a correlation between the two sets of scores?
- What type of design has been used: repeated measures? independent groups? matched pairs?
- What level of measurement is the data?
- If measurement is interval or ratio, are the other necessary criteria for the use of a parametric test met?
- Is the variability in the two sets of scores similar?
- Can it be assumed that the distribution of scores in the population is normal or is there a skew in the distribution of the scores?

There is a flow chart at the very end of the book that gives further help with test selection.

Decide what the most appropriate test would be to analyse the data collected in the following studies:

1 A student observes whether drivers with one or more children in the car or drivers without a child in the car are more likely to stop at a zebra crossing.
2 Male twenty-year-olds are asked to indicate their own body shape and the body shape they think women like most on an illustrated rating scale. The two sets of ratings are compared.
3 The ratings on the body scale that men think women prefer and that women actually say they prefer are compared.
4 A research study investigates the hypothesis that married couples will be of similar attractiveness by asking an opportunity sample of the general public to rate pictures of husbands and wives.
5 A researcher investigates whether there is a correlation between scores on a health questionnaire and on a scale measuring stress.
6 The digit span of participants under thirty years old and over seventy years old is compared.

Exercise 38

Section Twelve

- *When to use* and *how to calculate*
  Chi-square test
  Sign test
  Mann–Whitney test
  Wilcoxon signed ranks test
  t-test for unrelated data
  t-test for related data
  Spearman's rank order correlation coefficient
  Pearson's product moment correlation coefficient
- How to rank scores

The interpretation of test results is covered in Section Thirteen. If you are not familiar with interpreting the results of statistical tests, you will need to read this section first.

Tests for data at the nominal level

- Chi-square test
- Sign test

Chi-square test

When to use   The chi-square test is used if you have data at the *nominal level* (data in which you allocate participants to a category) and if the data is *independent* (each participant can only be represented in one 'cell' of the chart) or if *all* the observations come from the same participant.

It is important that you understand this last point. If you did a study in which you observed whether males and females fastened their coats and/or carried umbrellas if it rains, you might collect data like this:

	Males	Females
Fastened coats	12	24
Carried umbrellas	8	42
Neither	48	6

This might look like data suitable for a chi-square – but if some people fastened their coats *and* carried umbrellas, they would be counted in two 'cells'. Thus the data is not independent and chi-square is not appropriate.

Chi-square tests the *association* between the numbers in rows (which will represent one variable) and the numbers in the columns (which will represent another variable).

Rationale   Chi-square compares the numbers that you actually allocate to each category (the *observed frequencies*) with what would be expected if these numbers were distributed by chance (the *expected frequencies*).

Limitations in the use of chi-square

- Data must be the actual frequencies that you counted, not means, proportions, ratios, and so on.
- Data must be independent (see above, p. 157).
- Always use *two-tailed values* except in a 'goodness of fit' test (see later in this section, p. 157).
- When you calculate a chi-square you work out *expected frequencies*. If several of these are less than five, you increase the chance of concluding that there is an association between the variables when really there is not (see later in this section, p. 157). This is particularly likely to occur if your sample size is small.

Instructions for calculating a chi-square

1   Arrange the data in boxes or 'cells' following this pattern:

Example: Results of a study observing whether men and women carry a pile of books in different ways			
	Males	Females	Total
Carry books at side	17	4	21
Carry books in front	7	22	29
Total	24	26	50

The data that you have collected are called the *observed values* – abbreviated to *O*.

2   Calculate the expected frequency (*E*) for each cell, using the formula:

$$E = \frac{\text{total of the row} \times \text{total of the column}}{\text{overall total}}$$

Example: Results of a study observing whether men and women carry a pile of books in different ways

	Males	Females	Total
	Cell a	Cell b	
Carry books at side	17	4	21
	Cell c	Cell d	
Carry books in front	7	22	29
	24	26	50

For *Cell a*: $E = \dfrac{21 \times 24}{50} = 10.08$

For *Cell c*: $E = \dfrac{29 \times 24}{50} = 13.92$

Calculate E for *Cell b* and *Cell d*.[1]

3 Find the value of χ^2 from the formula $\chi^2 = \sum \dfrac{(O - E)}{E}$ where:

O = the observed frequency for that cell;

E = the expected frequency for that cell, and $\sum$ means 'sum of'.

Calculation on the above data: *Cell a* $= \dfrac{17 - 10.08}{10.08} = 4.75$

It keeps the calculation tidy if you use a table like this:

....

1 For *Cell b*: $E = \dfrac{21 \times 26}{50} = 10.92$

For *Cell d*: $E = \dfrac{29 \times 26}{50} = 15.08$

	O	E	O −E	$(O - E)^2$	$(O - E)^2/E$
Cell a	17	10.08	6.92	47.89	4.75
Cell b	4	10.92	−6.92	48.89	4.39
Cell c	7	13.92	−6.92	47.88	3.44
Cell d	22	15.08	6.92	47.89	3.18
				Total of $(O - E)^2/E$	= 15.76

Thus the observed value of chi-square in this example is 15.76.

4   Find the *degrees of freedom* (*df*) from the formula:

df = (number of rows − 1) × (number of columns − 1)

In the above example this will be $(2 - 1) \times (2 - 1) = 1$.

Degrees of freedom are quite complicated to explain. It concerns how much the observations collected are free to vary.

Example

If you observe your friend putting on their jeans, they can choose which leg to put in first. Having made this decision they are left with no choice over which leg to put in second! With only two categories in the choice, there is thus one degree of freedom.

If your friend was washing their dog's legs, they would have three degrees of freedom as to the order in which they did it. They have lots of choice as to which leg should be first, still choice for which should be second, limited choice as to which was to be third, and no choice as to which leg was washed last.

Looking up the significance in critical value table (Appendix Table 1)

As nominal categories are by definition unordered, it is not logical to make a directional (one-tailed) prediction about the direction of the results in an ordinary chi-square. (It is possible to use them in a 'goodness of fit' chi-square, as explained in the next section.) *Two-tailed values should always be used for the normal chi-square test.*

Find Table 1, 'Critical values of χ^2', in the appendix. The level of **significance** depends on the degrees of freedom. Find the appropriate line for your *df* and put something under this line. Put your finger where your value of chi-square would fit in. Take the column on the left of your finger and follow it up to the top. That is the level of significance for your study. (If there is nothing to the left it is non-significant.) For the example above:

	Levels of significance (p)				
	0.10	0.05	0.01	0.001	
df = 1	2.71	3.84	6.64	10.83	*
2	4.60	5.99	9.21	13.82	
Note : * indicates the point where 15.76 would fit in.					

As 15.76 is bigger than 10.83 the level of significance indicates that the probability that this is a chance result is less than 0.001 or 0.01 per cent ($p < 0.001$). Thus you could accept your experimental hypothesis – although there is still a small chance that the result is due to chance.

Quick 2 × 2 formula   This can only be used for a 2 × 2 test.

$$= \frac{n(ad \times bc)}{(a+b)(c+d)(a+c)(b+d)}$$

Where n = total sample size, a = observed value in *Cell a*, b = observed value in *Cell b*, and so on.

Some controversies over the use of chi-square

Yates' correction   Until recently statisticians argued that in a 2 × 2 chi-square 'Yates' correction' should be used. It now seems to be agreed that this is not essential, and so in the interests of simplicity it is not included here.

Low expected frequencies   Psychologists of my generation learnt by heart: 'Chi-square is not reliable if 20 per cent of the expected frequencies are less than five' – Cochran (1954). However, this issue has recently been researched by Coolican, who writes:

> The most uncontroversial position in contemporary research seems to be that *with a total sample of more than twenty*, the test can tolerate expected frequencies as low as one or two in one or two cells....*For total sample sizes less than twenty* and two expected cells below five, the risk of a Type I error is too high.
>
> (Coolican 1994: 266)

It seems to the present author that you must be cautious when interpreting the results of a chi-square with several E values below five. The result *may* indicate an association of some kind between the variables – but further research would be needed to be certain that such an association really exists.

'Goodness of fit' chi-square   This is a special type of chi-square when the distribution amongst categories on only one variable is being studied. For example:

Numbers in different age groups who like Brussel sprouts					
Age	1–5	6–10	11–15	16–20	21–25	Total
	0	2	14	25	29	70

An 'eyeball' test suggests older people are more likely to like sprouts. This hypothesis can be tested by a 'goodness of fit' test.

Calculating a 'goodness of fit' test

1   Calculate the expected frequencies (E) in each cell. If distribution was due to chance then the observed values should all be the same, so the expected frequency for each cell is the overall total divided by the number of cells. (In this case $E = 70 \div 5 = 14$.)

2   Calculate $\dfrac{(O - E)^2}{E}$ for each cell as before.

3   As before chi-square $= \sum \dfrac{(O - E)^2}{E}$.

Putting these values in a table as used earlier:

	O	E	O − E	(O − E)²	(O − E)²/E
Cell a	0	14	−14	196	14.00
Cell b	2	14	−12	144	10.29
Cell c	14	14	0	0	0
Cell d	25	14	11	121	8.64
Cell e	29	14	15	225	16.07
				Total	49.00

Thus the value of chi-square is 49.00

4   The degrees of freedom is the number of cells minus one:

($5 - 1 = 4$)

5   Look up the significance level using the table of critical values as before.

	Levels of significance (p)				
	0.10	0.05	0.01	0.001	
df = 3	6.25	7.82	11.34	16.27	
4	7.78	9.49	13.28	18.46	*
5	9.24	11.07	15.09	20.52	

Note: * indicates where our calculated value of chi-square (49) would be.

Move to the top of the column on the left – this gives a level of significance of 0.001. This means the probability that the result is due to chance is less than 0.1 per cent (p < 0.001). We can accept the experimental hypothesis that there is an association between liking sprouts and age – although there is still a small chance that we are wrong.

Sign test

When to use The sign test is used to test if there is a difference when you have data at the *nominal level* (data in which you have counted how many cases fall in each category) and you have a *related measures design* or a *matched pairs design*.

Example

You could use a sign test if you wanted to see if there are differences in attitudes towards a common European currency between people who travel abroad a lot and people (matched with the former on other characteristics) who have never been abroad.

Scores on an attitude questionnaire comparing the answers of matched pairs of participants, one who has never been abroad and one who travels abroad a great deal		
	Travel a lot	*Never been abroad*	*Direction of change*
Pair 1	18	14	+
Pair 2	15	15	=
Pair 3	17	10	+
Pair 4	16	12	+
Pair 5	19	17	+
Pair 6	16	17	−
Pair 7	14	10	+
Pair 8	17	17	=
Note: High score = positive attitude; maximum score = 20.		

You can see that in one pair the person who travels little is more in favour, in five cases the regular travellers are more in favour and in two cases there is no difference in attitude.

Rationale This very simple test compares the number of changes in one direction and the number of changes in the other direction with what would be expected by chance.

Instructions for calculating a sign test

1   Assign the change between Condition A and B a positive, negative or equal value, being careful always to allocate the sign in a consistent fashion.
2   Count up how many plus- and minus-signs you have allocated. The smaller of these values is the observed value for the test (S).
3   Count the number of participants who were assigned a sign other than zero (N).
4   Look up S in the critical value tables (Table 2 in the appendix).

Example

Table to show whether participants choose to wait alone or with others under stressful or non-stressful conditions			
	Stressful condition	Non-stressful condition	Direction of change
P1	With others	Alone	−
P2	With others	Alone	−
P3	Alone	With others	+
P4	With others	Alone	−
P5	With others	With others	0
P6	With others	Alone	−
P7	Alone	Alone	0
P8	With others	Alone	−
P9	With others	Alone	−
P10	With others	Alone	−

You can see that this gives us a total of:

plus-signs = 1, minus-signs = 7

This means that the value of S is 1.

Counting the number of participants with a sign other than zero, the value of N is 8.

Looking up the significance in critical value table (Appendix Table 2)

Along the top line you will see 'Levels of significance' labelled 'one-' or 'two-tailed'. If you have a directional hypothesis, use the one-tailed values; if you have a non-directional research hypothesis, use the two-tailed values.

The left-hand column is labelled 'N'. Find the appropriate line for your study and place something under the line so it is easy to follow. Put your finger on this line where your value of S would fit in. Take the column to the left and follow it to the top. That is the level of significance for your study. (If there is nothing to the left it is non-significant.)

For the examples above:

1   *How travellers and non-travellers react to the common European currency. $N = 6$; $S = 1$.*

Level of significance for a two-tailed test				
0.10	0.05	0.02	0.01	0.001
N = 6 0	0	–	–	–

As the calculated value of $S > 0$, the result is non-significant.

2   *Choice of waiting alone or with company. $N = 8$; $S = 1$.*

Level of significance for a two-tailed test				
0.01	0.05	0.02	0.01	0.001
N = 8 1	0	0	0	0

Thus the probability that the result is due to chance is $p < 0.10$ or 10 per cent. (For discussion of whether this would be regarded as significant, see Section Thirteen.)

Two sample tests for data at the ordinal level

- Mann–Whitney test
- Wilcoxon signed ranks test

Before calculating these tests you will need to know how to *rank* scores, as it is a characteristic of non-parametric tests such as these that they do not use the raw scores in the calculations but the rank of the scores.

Ranking

This procedure involves arranging the scores in order and then assigning them a number which reflects their position in that order.

Example

Eight students sit a test and their scores out of fifty are:

P1	34
P2	15
P3	44
P4	34
P5	22
P6	36
P7	18
P8	39

Step 1 Write down the scores in ascending order:

15 18 22 34 34 36 39 44

Step 2 Number each score, calling the lowest '1', the next '2', and so on. (If the last number doesn't match the number of scores you've missed one!)

15	18	22	34	34	36	39	44
1	2	3	4	5	6	7	8

When you do this it is a good idea to write the numbers underneath in a different colour to the original list.

Step 3 Often two or more of the original scores will be the same. These are called *tied ranks*. In the example above, two people scored 34 – it is obviously silly that one is numbered *4* and one *5*; they should both be the same rank.

If there are tied ranks like this, the rank given will be halfway between the two numbers which you have written below.

34	34	Half-way point between 4 and 5
4	5	= 4.5

Step 4 The ranks would be written out as:

15	18	22	34	34	36	39	44
1	2	3	4.5	4.5	6	7	8

(Note that only the numbers under the tied scores have changed.)

If you have three tied ranks, each will take the value of the middle rank:

Score	12	14	14	14	26	29
Number	1	2	3	4	5	6
Rank	1	3	3	3	5	6

Each score of 14 is given the middle rank from the group of numbers *2 3 4*, i.e. *3*.

However many tied scores you have they are always given the middle rank or the halfway point. For example, in:

10	12	12	12	12	12	14
1	2	3	4	5	6	7

all the 12s would be Rank *4*; and in:

3	3	3	4	5	6	7	7	7	7
1	2	3	4	5	6	7	8	9	10

all the 3s would be Rank *2* and all the 7s would be Rank *8.5*.

Step 5 When all the ranks have been worked out, write them on the original table:

Table of students' scores in the test and their rank orders		
	Test score	*Rank*
P1	34	*4.5*
P2	15	*1*
P3	44	*8*
P4	34	*4.5*
P5	22	*3*
P6	36	*6*
P7	18	*2*
P8	39	*7*

Exercise 39

Put the following sets of scores into rank order:

1   1, 2, 5, 5, 5, 7, 3, 4
2   10, 14, 13, 14, 10, 9, 13, 11, 12, 15
3   1, 3, 5, 1, 7, 3, 1, 8, 2, 1, 1
4   100, 122, 123, 112, 122, 103, 104
5   0.1, 0.2, 0.8, 0.2, 1.2, 0.05, 0.7, 0.2

The Mann–Whitney test

When to use The Mann–Whitney U-test is suitable when you have used an *independent groups design* and you have predicted that there will be a difference between the results of the two groups. It can be used on data measured on an *ordinal scale* and the test makes no assumptions about the shape of the population distribution.

Rationale The rationale behind the test is simple. If you collect data from two groups of participants and rank order all of the scores as if they were one big list, then, if the scores of the two groups are similar and any differences are chance differences, the rank orders that have been assigned to scores in each group will also be similar. However, if the scores of each group were different then there will be a preponderance of high ranks in one group and low ranks in the other group. Mann–Whitney works by comparing the ranks given to each group of participants.

Instructions for calculating the Mann–Whitney test

1 Rank *all* the scores for both groups as a single set of scores. (See pp. 162–4 if you do not know how to put scores in rank order.)
2 Add the total of the ranks for the first group and the total of the ranks for the second group separately.
3 Select the larger of the rank totals. (Call this *T*.)
4 Find the value of *U* from the formula:

$$U = n_1 n_2 + \frac{n_T(n_T + 1)}{2} - T$$

where:

n_1 = number of participants in first group
n_2 = number of participants in second group
T = largest rank total
n_T = number of participants in the group with the largest rank total

Example

Table to show recall of words by two groups: group 1 using imagery and group 2 using repetition to aid recall			
Group 1 scores	Rank	Group 2 scores	Rank
9	11	5	4.5
9	11	6	6.5
8	9	5	4.5
7	8	4	2.5
6	6.5	3	1
9	11	4	2.5
Total of ranks	56.5		21.5

In this example $n_1 = 6$; $n_2 = 6$; $T = 56.5$; $n_T = 6$, so:

$$U = 6 \times 6 + \frac{6(6+1)}{2} - 56.5 = 36 + \frac{42}{2} - 56.5 = 0.5$$

Looking up the significance in critical value table (Appendix Table 3)

Mann–Whitney tables are unlike the tables for other tests. If you turn to the appendix and look at Table 3, you will find that there is a different table for each level of significance. Start with Table 3d (headed 'Critical values of U for a one-tailed test at 0.05') if you have a directional hypothesis, or Table 3c (headed '...two-tailed test at 0.05') if your hypothesis is non-directional. Locate n_1 along the top and n_2 down the side. Where these two lines meet is the critical value of U for your study, and the calculated value of U must be equal to or less than this value to enable you to accept the experimental hypothesis.

Large samples (n_1 or n_2 < 20)

The tables of critical values for Mann–Whitney do not go above twenty, and if you have a sample larger than this you have to perform a *z transformation* using the formula:

$$z = \frac{U - \frac{n_1 n_2}{2}}{\sqrt{\frac{n_1 n_2 (n_1 + n_2 + 1)}{12}}}$$

z is then looked up in the appropriate table of critical values. If $z \geq$ 1.96, $p < 0.05$; if $z \geq 2.58$, $p < 0.01$.

You might wish to remember this when collecting data and restrict the number of participants used in your research!

Unequal numbers in the two groups

If you carry out a study which results in there being unequal numbers of participants in the two groups, you should calculate U for *both rank totals* (selecting the correct number for n_1 and n_2 as you do so) and then compare the smaller value of U with the numbers in the critical value tables.

Wilcoxon signed ranks test

Be careful not to just call this test the Wilcoxon test. Wilcoxon designed two tests that both bear his name. The Wilcoxon signed ranks test is also referred to as the Wilcoxon matched pairs signed ranks test and as the Wilcoxon T-test. (This is always written 'T' – in capitals. Be careful! It is easy to confuse it with the t-test, which is a very different beast.)

When to use The Wilcoxon signed ranks test is used when you have data at the *ordinal* level and you are testing to see if there is a *difference* between two sets of scores obtained from the same participants in a *repeated measures design* or from *matched pairs*.

Rationale In this test you begin by ranking the scores on each test separately, then you subtract the rank each participant gains on one test from their rank on the other test. The idea is that if nearly all the participants have done much better on one test than the other then nearly all these differences will be of the same sign ($+$ or $-$). However, if some participants have done better on one test and others have done worse, then the differences will be a mixture of signs.

Step-by-step instructions

1   Calculate the difference (*d*) between each pair of scores, noting if the difference is positive or negative.
2   Rank these differences *ignoring whether they are positive or negative* and omitting any zeros. Call the smallest difference Rank 1.
3   Add up the total of the ranks of the positively signed differences.
4   Add up the total of the negatively signed differences.
5   Take the smallest of the totals obtained in steps 3 and 4 as *T*.
6   Compare this number with the values in Appendix Table 4.

Example

You test ten participants in a repeated measures design, comparing memory for words using repetition or imagery.

Table to show the number of words recalled by participants using imagery and repetition				
	Imagery	*Repetition*	*d*	*Rank*
P1	10	6	−4	*7.5*
P2	9	6	−3	*5.5*
P3	8	8	0	
P4	9	8	−1	*2*
P5	7	8	+1	*2*
P6	9	9	0	
P7	6	8	+2	*4*
P8	10	7	−3	*5.5*
P9	9	5	−4	*7.5*
P10	10	9	−1	*2*
Note: Total of the positive ranks = 6.0				
Total of the negative ranks = 30.0				
Therefore *T* is 6.0				

Looking up the result in critical value table (Appendix Table 4)

Along the top line you will see levels of significance labelled 'one-tailed test' or 'two-tailed test'. Use the one appropriate to your experimental hypothesis.

The left-hand column is headed N. This stands for the number of pairs *not counting ties*. In the above example $N = 8$. Find the line for your N and place something under it so you don't get lost. Put your finger on the line where your particular value of T would fit in. Take the column to the left of your finger (or the actual column if your number is an exact match) and follow it to the top. That is the level of significance for your study. (If there is nothing to the left it is non-significant.)

For the above example:

	Levels of significance			
	0.05	0.025	0.01	0.005 (one-tailed)
N	0.10	0.05	0.02	0.01 (two-tailed)
8	6	4	2	0

As 6.0 actually appears on this line, the level of significance reached is $p = 0.05$ if you have a directional hypothesis, or $p = 0.10$ if you have a non-directional hypothesis. (The latter would normally be regarded as non-significant.)

Two sample tests for data fulfilling the requirements for the use of parametric tests

- *t*-test for unrelated (or independent) data
- *t*-test for related data

The t-test for unrelated data

When to use   The *t*-test for unrelated data is used when you have data of ordinal or interval level which also satisfies the other criteria for a parametric test, and you are testing to see if there is a *difference* between the scores of two groups which have *different* participants in them (i.e. you are using an *independent groups design*).

Rationale   The unrelated *t*-test compares the amount of variability between the two sets of scores with the overall variability in all the scores. Variability between the groups is calculated as a difference between the means. Total variability is calculated from the rather horrendous-looking bottom line of the formula, which takes into account the variability of individual scores from the group mean. It isn't as bad to calculate as it looks!

Instructions for calculating the value of t

1   Total the scores in Condition A and then calculate the mean for A.
2   Calculate the square of the total of the scores in Condition A.
3   Total the scores in Condition B and then calculate the mean for B.
4   Calculate the square of the total of the scores in Condition B.
5   Square each score in Condition A.
6   Calculate the total of these squared scores.
7   Square each score in Condition B.
8   Calculate the total of these squared scores.
9   Find the value of *t* from the formula:

$$t = \frac{M_1 - M_2}{\sqrt{\frac{\left(\sum x_1^2 - \frac{(\sum x_1)^2}{n_1}\right) + \left(\sum x_2^2 - \frac{(\sum x_2)^2}{n_2}\right)}{(n_1 - 1) + (n_2 - 1)}} \left(\frac{1}{n_1} + \frac{1}{n_2}\right)}$$

where:

M_1 = mean of Group A

M_2 = mean of Group B

$\sum x_1^2$ = sum of the squared scores in Group A

$\sum x_2^2$ = sum of the squared scores in Group B

$\left(\sum x_1\right)^2$ = sum of scores in Group A squared

$\left(\sum x_2\right)^2$ = sum of scores in Group B squared

n_1 = number of participants in Group A

n_2 = number of participants in Group B

It does not matter if the value of t *is positive or negative. When looking it up in the critical value table ignore the sign.*

10   Calculate the degrees of freedom (*df*) by adding the number of participants in Group A minus one to the number of participants in Group B minus one.

$$df = (n_1 - 1) + (n_2 - 1)$$

Example

One group of participants (Group A) are timed to see how long they take to solve an anagram of 'LUNCH' (CHUNL) at 9.00 AM and a second group (Group B) are timed to see how long they take to solve the same anagram at 12.00 noon. The directional hypothesis is that participants will solve an anagram of 'LUNCH' faster when it is nearly lunchtime than when it is early in the day.

	Group A (9.00 am)		Group B (12.00 am)	
	Scores	Squared scores	Scores	Squared scores
	10	100	2	4
	5	25	1	1
	6	36	7	49
	3	9	4	16
	9	81	4	16
	8	64	5	25
	7	49	2	4
	5	25	5	25
	6	36	3	9
	5	25	4	16
Total	64	450	37	165
Mean	6.4		3.7	

Number of seconds taken to solve the anagram 'CHUNL' at 9.00 am and 12.00 am

In this example,

$$t = \frac{6.4 - 3.7}{\sqrt{\frac{\left(450 - \frac{4096}{10}\right) + \left(165 - \frac{1369}{10}\right)}{9+9}\left(\frac{1}{10} + \frac{1}{10}\right)}}$$

$$= \frac{2.7}{\sqrt{\frac{(450 - 409.6) + (165 - 136.9)}{18} \times \frac{1}{5}}}$$

$$= \frac{2.7}{\sqrt{3.806 \times 0.2}} = \frac{2.7}{\sqrt{0.7612}}$$

$t = 3.096$

Looking up the significance in critical value table (Appendix Table 5)

Follow the same procedure as for the *t*-test for related data (described below).

In the above example, $t = 3.096$ and $df = (10 - 1) + (10 - 1) = 18$.

	Levels of significance			
	0.05	0.025	0.01	0.005 (one-tailed)
df	0.10	0.05	0.02	0.01 (two-tailed)
17	1.740	2.110	2.567	2.898
18	1.734	2.101	2.552	2.878 *
19	1.729	2.093	2.539	2.861

As our calculated value of *t* would fit at * and we have a directional hypothesis, the level of significance reached is 0.005. In other words the probability that the result is due to chance is 0.5 per cent ($p < 0.005$) so we can accept the experimental hypothesis – although as always there is a small chance that this is a chance result.

The t-test for related data

When to use The *t*-test for related data is used when you have data of *interval* or *ratio level* which also fulfils the other requirements for the use of a parametric test, and you are testing to see if there is a *difference* between two sets of scores obtained from the same participants in a *repeated measures design* or from *matched pairs*.

Rationale The test compares the differences between the two sets of scores with the total overall variability in the scores.

Instructions for calculating a t-test for related data

1 Calculate the differences between the score each person obtained in Condition A and Condition B. Make sure you always take A from B or B from A!

2 Add up these differences (counting minus scores as minuses).

3 Square these differences.

4 Add up the squared differences.

5 Square the total of the differences obtained in Step 2.

6 Find *t* from the formula:

$$t = \frac{\sum d}{\sqrt{\dfrac{N\sum d^2 - (\sum d)^2}{N-1}}}$$

where:

d = total of the differences between scores in A and B

$\sum d^2$ = total of the squared differences (Step 4)

$(\sum d)^2$ = the differences totalled and then squared (Step 5)

N = the number of participants

$\sqrt{\ }$ = take the square root

7 Calculate the degrees of freedom. In this case the number of participants minus one ($df = N - 1$).

There are different versions of this formula so don't worry if you find another that looks different.

Example

Suppose you persuade your local weightwatchers club to compare the effects of dieting for a month with increased exercise for a month. The results are as follows:

	Low-fat diet	Increased exercise	d	d^2
P1	10	2	8	64
P2	5	1	4	16
P3	6	7	−1	1
P4	3	4	−1	1
P5	9	4	5	25
P6	8	5	3	9
P7	7	2	5	25
P8	5	5	0	0
P9	6	3	3	9
P10	5	4	1	1
Total	64	37	27	151
Mean	6.4	3.7		

$$t = \frac{27}{\sqrt{\frac{10 \times 151 - (27)^2}{10 - 1}}} = \frac{27}{\sqrt{\frac{1510 - 729}{9}}}$$

$$= \frac{27}{\sqrt{86.8}} = \frac{27}{9.315} = 2.89 \text{ (to 2 decimal places)}$$

Looking up the significance in critical value table (Appendix Table 5)

At the top you will see the levels of significance labelled 'one-tailed' and 'two-tailed'. Choose the one appropriate to your experimental hypothesis.

The left-hand column is headed *df* for 'degrees of freedom'. Find the right *df* (as calculated in Step 7) for your study, and place something under this so you don't get lost. Put your finger on this line where your value of *t* would fit in. Take the column to the left of your finger (or the actual column if your number is an exact match) and follow it up to the top. That is the level of significance for your study. (If there is nothing to the left of your finger the result is non-significant.)

For the example above, where *t* = 2.89 and *df* = 9

	Levels of significance				
	0.05	0.025	0.01	0.005	(one-tailed)
df	0.10	0.05	0.02	0.01	(two-tailed)
8	1.860	2.306	2.896	3.355	
9	1.833	2.262	2.821 *	3.250	
10	1.812	2.228	2.764	3.169	

The calculated value of t would fit at *. Thus, for our non-directional hypothesis, the level of significance reached is 0.02. In other words the probability that this is a chance result is 2 per cent ($p < 0.02$) and we could accept our experimental hypothesis – although there would still be a 2 per cent chance that the result was actually due to chance.

Tests for correlation

For data at the ordinal level of measurement:

• Spearman's rank order correlation coefficient

For data that fulfils the requirements for the use of a parametric test:

• Pearson's product moment correlation coefficient

Spearman's rank order correlation coefficient

(This test is sometimes referred to as Spearman's rho.)

When to use This is a *non-parametric* test which measures the amount of *correlation* between two sets of scores. To use it you need to have data at the *ordinal* level of measurement, and to be testing to see if there is a *relationship* between the sets of scores.

Rationale   In the Spearman test the scores on each variable are ranked and the test compares the rank each person is given in each condition. If there is a *positive correlation* between the two variables then people who are ranked high on one will also be ranked high on the other. If there is a *negative correlation* then people who are ranked high on one will be ranked low on the other. If there is no relationship (or a chance distribution of scores) then the ranks will all be mixed up.

When you are investigating whether there is a correlation between variables draw a scattergram. This will give an indication of the nature *of the relationship between the scores which, if it is 'U-shaped', will not be shown by the result of an inferential test.*

Instructions for calculating the value of rho

1   Rank the scores on variable *A*. Give Rank 1 to the smallest score.
2   Rank the scores on variable *B* in the same way.
3   Calculate the difference (*d*) between each pair of ranks.
4   Square each of the differences calculated in Step 3 (d^2).
5   Add up the total of these squares ($(\sum d^2)$).
6   Count the number of participants (*N*).
7   Find the value of rho (*r*) from the following formula:

$$r_s = 1 - \frac{6 \sum d^2}{N(N^2 - 1)}$$

Example

You investigate whether there is a relationship between the number of hours of paid work a student does each week and their end of year exam score.

Participant	Hours worked per week	Rank	Exam score (max. 100)	Rank	d	d^2
1	6	6	60	6.5	0.5	0.25
2	0	3	64	8	5.0	25.00
3	12	9	55	3.5	5.5	30.25
4	0	3	55	3.5	0.5	0.25
5	20	10	40	1.5	8.5	72.25
6	10	8	60	6.5	1.5	2.25
7	0	3	70	10	7.0	49.00
8	0	3	65	9	6.0	36.00
9	0	3	40	1.5	0.5	0.25
10	8	7	58	5	2.0	4.00
Total						219.50

Table to show the hours of paid work and exam scores of students

$$r = 1 - \frac{6 \times \sum d^2}{N(N^2 - 1)} = 1 - \frac{6 \times 219.5}{10(100 - 1)} = -0.330$$

Looking up the significance in critical value table (Appendix Table 6)

Along the top line you will see the levels of significance for one- and two-tailed tests. If you have a directional hypothesis (i.e. you have said there will be a *positive* or a *negative* correlation between your two variables) then you use the one-tailed significance levels. If you have a non-directional hypothesis (i.e. you have just said that there will be a correlation) then you will use the two-tailed significance levels.

The left-hand column is headed *N* for 'number of subjects'. Find the right number for the study and place something under this line to make it easy to find. (If your number of *N* is not there then take the next smallest.) Put your finger on this line where your particular value of rho (r) would fit in. Take the column to the *left* of your finger (or the actual column if your number is an exact match) and follow it up to the top. That is the level of significance for your study. (If there is nothing to the left then it is non-significant.)

For the example above:

N	Levels of significance				
	0.05	0.025	0.01	0.005	(one-tailed)
	0.10	0.05	0.02	0.01	(two-tailed)
10	0.564	0.648	0.745	0.794	

-0.330 would have nothing to the left and so this would be a non-significant result; you would retain the null hypothesis.

When there are tied ranks

If several participants gain the same score on one variable so that there are tied ranks, there is a tendency for results derived from the Spearman formula to be inflated. Siegel (1956) states that if the proportion of ties is not large, their effect on the value of rho is negligible, but if the proportion of ties is large the result will be unreliable (see Siegel 1956: 206–10 for a full discussion). Coolican suggests (1994: 304) that a Pearson calculation should be conducted on the scores if any values are tied.

Pearson's product moment correlation coefficient

When to use   This is a test for the amount and significance of a *correlation* between people's scores on two variables, which requires the data to be measured on an *interval* or *ratio* scale and to meet the other assumptions of parametric tests.

Rationale   The test is designed to test if high scores on one variable are matched by high scores on the other variable, but also has to take into account the fact that the variables may be measured on different scales.

Step-by-step instructions

1 For each participant multiply the score on variable a by the score on variable b.
2 Total the results of Step 1.
3 Square the individual scores on variable a and then calculate the sum of these squared scores.
4 Square the individual scores on variable b and then calculate the sum of these squared scores.
5 Find the value of r from the formula:

$$r = \frac{N\sum a \times b - \sum a \times \sum b}{\sqrt{\left(N\sum a^2 - (\sum a)^2\right)\left(N\sum b^2 - (\sum b)^2\right)}}$$

where:

N = the number of participants
$a \times b$ = the total of the $a \times b$ column
a and b = the totals for each variable
$(\Sigma a)^2$ = total the scores on variable a then square it
$(\Sigma b)^2$ = total the scores on variable b then square it
Σa^2 = total all the squared scores on variable a
Σb^2 = total all the squared scores on variable b

Example

Supposing we wish to test the correlation between children's scores on a maths test and an English test.

Scores on a maths test and an English test for eight children				
	Maths score (a)	English score (b)	$a \times b$	a^2	b^2
P1	10	8	80	100	64
P2	12	10	120	144	100
P3	8	8	64	64	64
P4	9	11	99	81	121
P5	10	7	70	100	49
P6	8	11	88	64	121
P7	11	12	132	121	144
P8	7	7	49	49	49
Total	75	74	702	723	712

Thus $N = 8$; $a \times b = 702$; $a = 75$; $b = 74$; $(\Sigma a)^2 = 5{,}625$; $(\Sigma b)^2 = 5{,}476$; $\Sigma a^2 = 723$; $\Sigma b^2 = 712$.

$$r = \frac{(8 \times 702) - (75 \times 74)}{(8 \times 723 - 5{,}625)(8 \times 712 - 5{,}476)} = \frac{5{,}616 - 5{,}550}{159 \times 220}$$

$= 0.00189$ (to 5 decimal places)

Looking up the result in critical value table (Appendix Table 7)

Along the top you will see levels of significance for one- or two-tailed tests. Use the one which is appropriate for your research hypothesis.

The left-hand column is headed *df* for 'degrees of freedom'. For this test $df = N - 2$ (i.e. the number of pairs of scores minus two). Find the appropriate line and place something under it so you don't get lost. Put your finger where your value for *r* would fit in. Take the column to the left (or the actual column if your number is an exact match) and follow it to the top. That is the level of significance for your study. (If there is nothing to the left it is non-significant.)

For the above example:

	Levels of significance			
	0.05	0.025	0.01	(one-tailed)
	0.10	0.05	0.02	(two-tailed)
$df = N - 2$				
8	0.5494	0.6319	0.7155	

As 0.354 is smaller than all of these, we must retain the null hypothesis. Any correlation between maths and English results is due to chance.

Section Thirteen

- Interpreting test results
- Levels of significance
- Type I and Type II errors

Interpreting the results of a statistical test

The purpose of using inferential statistical tests is to enable you to estimate the probability that the result you have obtained has occurred due to chance.

- When you work out a test you obtain the *observed value* for that test for your data. For example chi-square = 3.78, rho = 0.456, $t = 1.234$ and so on.
- You then compare this *observed value* with the values given in *critical value tables*. How this is done is described in Section Twelve.
- The critical value tables give you an estimate of the probability that your result occurred due to chance.

How do they do that?   The top of the critical value table will look something like this:

Level of significance for a one-tailed test			
0.10	0.05	0.025	0.01
Level of significance for a two-tailed test			
0.20	0.10	0.05	0.02

What does this mean?   'Level of significance' indicates the probability that the results that you obtained in your research occurred on a chance basis. Put into jargon:

Levels of significance indicate the probability that you are making a Type I error (i.e. that you are saying you can accept your alternative/experimental hypothesis when the result is really due to chance). (For further discussion of Type I and II errors see later in this section.)

In other words if the critical value table indicates that for your result the level of significance is 0.10, this means there is a 10 per cent or 1 in 10 probability that your result was a chance effect. (To turn 0.10 to 10 per cent, just move the decimal point two places to the right.) If the level of significance indicated is 0.05, this means there is a 5 per cent or 1 in 20 probability that your results are a chance effect; 0.02 would indicate a 2 per cent or 1 in 50 probability that the results are a chance effect and so on.

Exercise 40

Turn these levels of significance into percentages and ratios:

0.01   0.025   0.20   0.001   0.005

An important point that should be emphasised here is that, when we are talking about a result being 'significant' and concluding that because of this we can accept our alternative (or experimental) hypothesis, we are always quoting a percentage probability that the result actually occurred on a chance basis. For example, if you conclude that your result reaches the 0.05 level of significance you are actually saying that there is a 5 per cent chance that your result is a chance effect – and thus there is a 5 per cent chance that your null hypothesis is actually correct!

In psychological research there is virtually always a small probability that your result is really a chance result, so there can never be 100 per cent certainty that what you found was due to alterations in the independent variable as predicted in your alternative (or experimental) hypothesis. The most we can usually say is that the probability that our result is down to chance is so small that we are prepared to risk accepting the alternative (or experimental) hypothesis.

At what level of significance can we accept the alternative hypothesis?

If the probability that our result is due to chance is 'low enough', we can accept the alternative hypothesis…but what is 'low enough'? A level of 0.10 or 10 per cent? of 0.05 or 5 per cent? or of 0.01 or 1 per cent?

In social science the 0.05 or 5 per cent level has become the accepted standard. If your results reach this level it is the convention that you can accept the alternative hypothesis.

Why choose the 5 per cent level?

This is all a question of the risk that we are prepared to take that our conclusions are wrong. As explained above, if we state that 'As the 5 per cent level of significance was reached the alternative hypothesis was accepted and the null hypothesis was rejected', we are actually saying that we will assume that our alternative hypothesis was correct – *but that there is still a 5 per cent chance that it is wrong.*

In social science – possibly because it is thought that nothing too terrible is going to happen if we are wrong – it is usual to call a difference or a correlation significant if it reaches the 5 per cent level. However choosing a significance level is always a matter of deciding the odds that you are prepared to accept of making a Type I error and rejecting the null hypothesis (which, of course, states that there is no difference or no correlation) when it is really correct.

If you wrongly accept or reject an alternative hypothesis when you are doing coursework, there are not going to be any disastrous consequences: thus the 5 per cent level is quite acceptable. Suppose, however, you are a research scientist working for a government department which was going to bring in a radical new way of treating paedophiles if your research suggested that the new measure was going to be effective. In such a case you might want to set a more stringent level of significance to be reached – perhaps 1 per cent or 0.1 per cent – before you were prepared to advise the government that they should implement the changes.

In some other cases you might be prepared to set a more lenient level of significance. For example if you were conducting a pilot study to see if it was likely to be worth carrying out a large-scale study, you might be happy to set a significance level of 10 per cent. This would indicate that there *may* be a difference or a correlation between your sets of scores – and that it is worth continuing with further research. When carrying out the full-scale research project, you would set a more stringent level.

Students sometimes find it confusing that the *smaller* the level of significance appears to be, the *greater* the probability that your alternative hypothesis is correct! Thus a level of 0.01 is *more* significant than one of 0.05. If you think about this a little it should become clear:

- A level of 0.05 means that there is a 5 per cent probability (or a 1 in 20 chance) that the result is due to chance.
- A level of 0.01 means that there is only a 1 per cent probability (or a 1 in a 100 chance) of a chance result.

Thus to accept your research hypothesis, the risk you are wrong is 5 per cent in the former case and only 1 per cent in the latter.

Exercise 41

1 Place the following levels of significance in order, starting with the least significant level:

   0.02   0.01   0.10   0.05   0.002   0.001

2 Which of the above levels is the most lenient?
3 Which of the above levels is the most stringent?

Type I and Type II errors

A Type I error occurs when we accept the alternative hypothesis when really we should retain the null hypothesis. We conclude that our results were significant when really they were not. A Type I error can occur:

- Because an experiment is badly designed and the result that has been obtained is actually due to the influence of confounding variables.
- Because the levels of significance that have been set are too *lenient*.

A **Type II error** occurs when we retain the null hypothesis (we retain the idea that the result is due to chance) when really we could accept the alternative hypothesis – we conclude that our results were due to chance when really they were not. There are two reasons for such errors:

- Because an experiment is badly designed and the result that has been obtained is actually due to the influence of confounding variables.
- Because the levels of significance that have been set are too *stringent*.

With a Type I error you conclude that there *is* a difference or that there *is* a correlation when really there *isn't*. This can occur because the level of significance set is too lenient. (Type I: 'I' looks like 'l' for lenient.)

With a Type II error you conclude that there *isn't* a difference or that there *isn't* a correlation when really there *is*. This can occur because the level of significance set is too stringent. (Type II: '2' looks like a backwards 'S' for stringent.)

If you set the level of significance that must be reached before you will reject the null hypothesis at 0.10 (10 per cent), this is an easier level to reach than 0.05 (5 per cent) – that is it is more *lenient*. You are saying you will accept the alternative hypothesis when there is actually a 10 per cent chance that the result is a chance occurrence. There is thus a greater risk of making a Type I error.

If you set the level of significance at 0.01 (1 per cent), this is a more difficult level to reach than 0.05 (5 per cent) – that is it is more *stringent*. You are saying you will accept the alternative hypothesis only if statistics show there is a mere 1 per cent probability that the result is a chance occurrence. There is thus a greater risk of making a Type II error.

At what point in the research do you set the level of significance that you will accept?

It has always been seen as good practice that you set the significance level that must be reached in order to accept the alternative hypothesis *before* you conduct the study. This will usually be set at the 0.05 or 5 per cent level. *If you set any other level you should justify your choice.*

What if I set the level at 5 per cent but the statistics show there is only a 1 per cent chance the result is due to chance?

This is a controversial area. Purists argue that if you set the level of significance at 5 per cent before you began the study you should only report if the results reach that 5 per cent level or not. You don't mention any other levels. Pragmatists argue that this is rather silly. They say: 'Why not report that your result not only reaches the 5 per cent level but also goes further than this and reaches the 1 per cent level?' In practice most academics writing in journals seem to be pragmatists not purists, and report the most stringent level of probability that their results reach.

Whichever line you choose to follow when writing up coursework will be accepted by an exam board.

How is the significance level which is reached expressed?

You will see expressions such as '$p < 0.05$' and '$p < 0.001$'.

If your result reaches the 0.05 level of significance in the critical value table, you will write that you are accepting the alternative hypothesis and that $p < 0.05$. This is shorthand for: 'If the null hypothesis is true, the probability of obtaining this result is less than 5 per cent'. In the same way $p < 0.001$ stands for: 'If the null hypothesis is true, the probability of obtaining this result is less than 0.1 per cent'.

Speaking strictly, 'p' stands for 'if the null hypothesis is true, the probability of obtaining this result is...'! Although it is rather a mouthful, try to memorise this phrase as it will gain you full marks if you are asked to explain $p < 0.05$, $p < 0.001$, etc. in an exam.

Conclusion

- If you are using inferential statistics, you calculate the result of your chosen test and obtain an observed value.
- You compare this calculated value with the critical value in the appropriate critical value table.
- This indicates the level of significance that your results reach – in other words the probability that your result is a chance occurrence.

- If this level is 5 per cent or less, it is usual to accept the alternative hypothesis – *but you should always bear in mind that there is still a certain chance that your null hypothesis is in fact correct.* If you state that you are accepting your alternative hypothesis because there is only a 5 per cent probability that the result is due to chance, you are also saying that there is still a 5 per cent probability that your null hypothesis is correct!

Section Fourteen

Interpreting qualitative research

If you are studying other science subjects, the qualitative approach may seem strange to you. If you conduct a pure qualitative study, you collect data from interviews, diary studies, observations, etc. but *you do not turn it into numbers of any kind.* To anyone educated within the empirical tradition of the scientific method, it is almost automatic to start counting and codifying things – but, of course, as soon as you do you are using quantitative methods.

If you dislike statistics the whole idea of qualitative research may sound very appealing (psychology without statistics? great!). Take care if this is your view. Good qualitative research requires a deep understanding of the topic being studied, understanding of your own subjective biases regarding that topic and even perhaps an understanding of what is being rejected in the quantitative approach. It is not an easy option. *Don't choose a qualitative study just because you dislike figures!*

In general there are two ways in which qualitative data is used in psychology:

- It can be used in conjunction with traditional quantitative research to expand and illustrate the findings: you could ask participants in an experiment what they thought the study was about and whether this influenced their answers; you could observe their behaviour and the style of language they use. For example, in his famous obedience study, Milgram (1963) comments that he regards it as significant that some compliant participants continued to call the experimenter 'Sir' throughout.
- It is also possible to see qualitative data as valuable in its own right, and to argue that a purely qualitative study will produce a richness of data, plus detailed information on the participants' individual and subjective viewpoints, which is lost in empirical studies.

If you collect qualitative data do not assume that it does not need some kind of analysis. When conducting qualitative research you will have an *aim*, just as with any other research – so you cannot just write down a list of things that were said by someone and submit this as your results! The data must be analysed and presented in a way that relates it to your aim in conducting the study.

There are various types of analysis that can be used. Two examples are:

- *Categorising.* Is it possible to group replies or observations together? Do several interviewees make similar points? Can this be related to their backgrounds or circumstances? Such categories can be imposed by the researcher from their own perspective, or categories may emerge from what the participants themselves say or do.
- *Selection of examples from the raw data.* Can you select certain quotations or examples of observations which typify a certain perspective?

Here is an example from the work of Smith (1995), describing how he analysed a case study on pregnancy and the transition to motherhood. He studied a small group of women using diary records, interviews and repertory grids, visiting each woman four times. Here are extracts from his comments on analysis:

> There is not one correct method for analysing qualitative material. One has to find a way of working which is appropriate to the material and to your own personal and theoretical propensity....I began by reading the transcripts...until I was very familiar with the material, using one margin to note my responses [to the text]...[and] the other margin to document emerging themes. On a separate sheet I listed the emerging themes and I looked for connections between them....I then turned to the second interview transcript and annotated in a similar way...this was repeated for interviews three and four. I found it useful to plot the themes on a 'time × category matrix' entering a summary statement for a theme for each cell. Material from the diary was inserted...in the matrix. Once I had achieved this conceptual schema for a case, I began a draft write-up...[making] constant reference back to the original transcripts.
>
> (Smith 1995: 122–5)

This procedure was repeated for each woman.

I am sure that you can see from this, that a qualitative study requires detailed understanding of the topic area and will involve a lengthy analysis of the material.

The very nature of qualitative research means that it is difficult to replicate and so there may be problems of *reliability*. Sometimes more than one rater or judge is used to check whether they agree on the interpretation of the findings. Some researchers will go back to the participants after the material has been analysed to check that *they* agree with the interpretation that has been made of what they did or said. (The following section covers reliability and validity.)

Reliability and validity

The issues of reliability and validity apply to qualitative research just as they do to quantitative studies.

Reliability   Can be checked by:

- *Triangulation.* This refers to the use of more than one technique of data collection, so that results using one method can be compared with those using the others. For instance, in the above example, Smith used interviews, diary entries and repertory grids.
- *Repetition.* Another check on reliability is to repeat the research, so that the initial conclusions can be re-examined several times.
- *One or more judges.* A further check is to use more than one rater or judge and compare the two sets of results to check the *inter-judge reliability.*

Validity   Can be checked by:

- *Consulting participants.* Do they agree with your conclusions?
- *Considering exceptions.* Taking into account the cases which *don't* fit your conclusions. It is important that you are open about the data which was collected and don't try to hide material which is awkward to explain. Other people can then consider whether they accept your explanations or not.
- *Definition of terms.* There must be careful definition of the factors being studied before the study begins. Whatever you are studying you have to define it so you know what you are looking at! How can you study 'attachment', 'aggression' or 'fear' if you haven't fully considered what the word means to you? (See the section below on observational studies for further discussion of this point.)

Another issue to consider is the extent to which your own beliefs and values will affect the conclusions you draw. You will need to carefully consider which of your own attitudes are of relevance to the area of study and to make these explicit. For example in Griffin's 1985 study of Birmingham schoolgirls, she makes it clear that she is undertaking the study from a feminist viewpoint. As it is part of the underlying philosophy of the qualitative approach that it is virtually impossible to be an objective observer of other human beings, this is an important consideration. You have to understand your own biases and how these will affect your analysis of the material, before you can conduct a good qualitative study.

It is probably the case that a completely qualitative study is beyond the competence of most A-level students. You may, indeed, find that your teachers also have little experience of the use of such methods. *This is not to say that you should not consider using qualitative data.* One way in which you can include such material is in conjunction with quantitative data. When conducting your research you could ask the participants what they think the study is about, what their attitude is to any ethical issues and so on. Such a use of qualitative data will greatly enrich an empirical study, and give you experience of using qualitative material in a small but still valuable way.

Another useful exercise is to conduct a small qualitative study as a class exercise. This will help you understand the advantages and difficulties of such research.

1 Explain the difference between qualitative and quantitative data. (This is also covered in Section Three.)
2 Describe two methods that could be used to analyse qualitative data from diary studies.

Exercise 42

Interpreting observational studies

As has already been explained, the data collected from an observational study can vary from strictly coded quantitative material to more subjective qualitative material.

Quantitative data

If quantitative data is being collected it is important that the criteria used are reported, so that:

- it can be seen that the categorisations made have a sound basis, and
- it would be possible for someone else to repeat the data-gathering process.

This means that you need to explain how you coded and scored the data you collected.

Quantitative data gathered in this way may well be suitable for analysis using inferential statistics; descriptive statistics – especially graphical techniques – are commonly used to present the material.

Qualitative data

If qualitative data is being reported this will often be in the form of detailed descriptions of behaviour. Here is an example from Piaget's work on the development of imitation:

> At 4 mos. 23 days…I showed L. my hand which I was slowly opening and closing. She seemed to be imitating me. All the time my suggestion lasted she kept up a similar movement and either stopped or did something else as soon as I stopped.…But was this response of L. merely an attempt at prehension [grasping]? To test this I then showed her some other object. She again opened and closed her hand…then immediately tried to seize the object.…I resumed the experiment with my hand and she clearly imitated it, her gesture being quite different from the one she made on seeing the toy.
>
> (Piaget 1951: 23)

You will find that Piaget's books have many examples of such detailed observations, from which he derived hypotheses for testing in other ways. The material needs to be sufficiently detailed that questions we might wish to ask about the event are answered in the description.

An important consideration with observational studies is their *internal validity*. In other words you must be careful that you really are measuring what you think you are measuring. This involves careful definition of variables and careful selection of the behaviours to be studied. For example if you were studying aggression, you would have to think very carefully about how to define this behaviour. Would you include aggression towards inanimate objects? or socially sanctioned aggression as might arise playing sport? Your study would lack validity if your measures of aggression did not meet the criteria used in your definition.

The *reliability* of the findings is another issue that should be considered when interpreting them. Was there a check of inter-observer reliability? Is the study replicable?

All such issues are relevant when considering the conclusions drawn from observational studies.

It may sound very tempting to conduct an observational study – it may even seem an easy option. This is far from the truth! Observational studies need to be *very* carefully planned and executed. If well done, however, they can produce a richness of data which is not found in laboratory work and so can be extremely interesting and valuable. When it comes to analysing the data, a very wide range of methods can be used depending on the data.

How might you analyse observational studies which had collected:

- simple nominal data – such as 'Did the baby cry out? Yes/No';
- ordinal data – such as 'Rate the cry on the following scale':

| Urgent | 5 | 4 | 3 | 2 | 1 | Non-urgent |

- interval data – such as the length of time the baby spent crying;
- qualitative data – such as data on the nature of the cry, how the baby looked while crying, how the baby reacted when picked up, and so on.

Exercise 43

Content analysis

Content analysis frequently involves the collection of quantitative data, as it involves counting how often a particular item is found in the material under scrutiny. As stated earlier, it is a variation on the observational technique, the material being observed being something from the media, a speech, a document and so on. It is likely that the material will be presented using graphical techniques and statistical tests.

Internal validity is a relevant issue, as a content analysis is only as good as the coding system that is used. The definitions on which the coding system is based and how it is operationalised need to be clearly explained so that the reader can judge for themselves whether any bias may have crept in. The study will probably be replicable, so it is possible to check the *reliability* of the findings, and a good content analysis will have built this into the study (for example, more than one judge will have been used and the *inter-judge reliability* will have been checked). The extent to which these factors have been satisfied need to be considered when interpreting the findings.

Discourse analysis

Discourse analysis refers to the analysis of communication between people. There is analysis of what is actually said, but also of the underlying biases behind the communication. For example, which words are chosen, 'racial cleansing' or 'genocide'? Are there variations in the manner of speaking when someone discusses different topics, rapid speech about a TV cookery programme but slower speech with several pauses and hesitations when discussing a programme on racial prejudice? Are there similar variations *between* speakers? How are alternative points of view dealt with?

Potter and Wetherall, who use this technique, state that:

Much of the work of discourse analysis is a craft skill...which is not easy to render or describe in a codified manner. Indeed as the analyst becomes more practised it becomes harder and harder to identify explicit procedures that could be called analysis.

(1987: 54)

In other words discourse analysis is a subtle art – and not an easy one.

Interpreting interviews

As with observational studies, because there are many different types of interview (see Section Three) there are many different methods by which the findings can be interpreted. Whatever the method that has been used, the results must be related back to the aim of the study.

- Structured interviews may have collected pure *quantitative data* at the nominal or ordinal level, and the researcher will use inferential statistics to analyse the results.
- Unstructured interviews may have collected *qualitative data*. It is not enough just to present the transcripts of the interviews as 'results', however. You need to interpret your findings in accordance with the aim of your research. This requires very great care. If you are going to select quotations or paraphrase material, you must take great care that the selection/paraphrasing does not lead to biased reporting. As with the analysis of any qualitative data, you will probably *categorise* the findings in some way. This involves grouping items together and, again, care must be taken that the researcher is interpreting what was said correctly. Some researchers go back to the interviewee after they have analysed the results to check that the way the material has been interpreted fits with what was intended.

When interpreting the findings of unstructured interviews there may be problems with *reliability* because the interviews are not replicable. This disadvantage, however, is countered by the additional richness of the data collected.

Interpreting case studies

All case studies are unique and so it is difficult to generalise as to how they should be interpreted. Case studies are likely to have included interviews and/or observations, and so everything written about these early in this section would apply. They are very likely to include *qualitative data*, such as self reports. This means that the interpretation of a case study can be very complex.

Another factor that needs to be considered is whether you are attempting to be an *objective* reporter. This again is a difficult issue. Is it possible to be objective when studying other people, or will your own *subjective* biases inevitably affect your reporting? (See 'Interpreting qualitative research' at the beginning of this section.)

Interpreting case studies is often highly complex. It is important that the findings are presented in such a way that they make clear the distinctions between:

• what actually happened/was said
• interpretations and inferences drawn by the participant(s)
• interpretations and inferences drawn by the researcher(s)

You need to make these distinctions between *objective* and *subjective* presentation clear, so that readers can make up their own minds as to whether or not they agree with the interpretation. If you re-read Piaget's description of his daughter earlier in this section, you will see that it is possible to isolate what L. actually did and how Piaget interprets her behaviour. As no two case studies are ever the same, *reliability* (the consistency of the findings) poses problems when interpreting the results because replication is impossible.

Conclusion

You can probably see by now that there are no hard-and-fast rules as to how to interpret the data obtained when using non-experimental methods. It all depends on the aim of the study, the nature of the study and the nature of the data that is collected. I have tried to indicate some of the issues that are involved, but for further information you should refer to a specialist text on the relevant method – and this is really beyond what is expected of a student pre-Higher Education.

Section Fifteen

- Brief advice on writing reports of your research

Writing reports

Before you begin, if it is possible, ask if you can have a look at reports from a previous year so that you can see how they were laid out. If this is not possible you may be able to find an example of a research report in a textbook. They are probably divided into the following sections:

- abstract or summary
- introduction
- aims/hypotheses
- method
- results
- treatment of results
- discussion
- conclusion
- references
- appendices

Title

Try to think of something short but informative. 'Perception of body shape' is a bit too lacking in information. 'Differences in the perception of body shape between males and females' would be better.

Abstract

This should summarise what you did, what you found and the conclusions. It should not be too long – 200 words is usually enough. It should state (concisely) the *area* of the study, its *aim* and/or *hypothesis*, the *research method/design*, the *participants*, the *results* found and the *conclusions* drawn. *Although this is the first section, write it last – it will be much easier.*

Introduction

This should contain *relevant* background material and previous research, leading to an *explanation of why the present study is being done* and ending with an explanation of the precise *aim* of the research and (if appropriate) your *hypotheses*. Only include material which focuses on what you are studying. Coolican (1994) suggests that the introduction can be seen as a funnel:

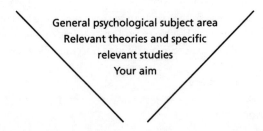

General psychological subject area
Relevant theories and specific
relevant studies
Your aim

- Explain applicable background theory and research.
- Outline how your ideas developed.
- Explain your exact aim.
- Explain how you formulated your hypotheses (including an explanation of why a directional or non-directional hypothesis was chosen).

- Finally state your research/experimental hypothesis and your null hypothesis (if appropriate).

Method

This should *describe exactly what was done* in your study. The criteria which has been used at coursework moderation meetings is that your explanation should be sufficiently clear and well-detailed to enable your granny to replicate the research. (This is obviously ageist and sexist: I apologise to any grannies reading this book – I hope to be one myself some day!)

The method section is divided into four sub-sections:

Design

Include the following:

- What research method did you use and why?
- What design was used? Why was this chosen?
- What are the IV and the DV (if appropriate)?
- What controls were used?
- Are there any relevant ethical issues?

Participants

- How many participants were used? Report age and gender if relevant.
- What sampling method was used?
- How were participants allocated to conditions?
- Who were the researchers?

Materials

- Report any apparatus used.
- Explain the origin of any materials used (such as word lists, questionnaires, etc.). Include *examples* of these (not all of them) in an appendix.
- Explain any scoring system used.

Procedure

Give granny a fighting chance here! Explain what you did so that she could replicate the study. This should include details of standardised instructions and procedures.

Results

The best reports usually present a summary of the results in the form of a table, then graphical representations and include raw data in an appendix. They also talk the reader through the findings, explaining what each element shows. They *don't* include twenty-five multi-coloured graphs which all show roughly the same thing! All the tables and graphs must be well-labelled, and for qualitative data there should still be a summary of some kind in the results – not just the entire unedited transcript.

Treatment of results

This section should explain what means of analysis were used and why. If you have used a statistical test you should explain why you chose that test. Finish the section with the calculated value of the statistic, the critical value for the number of participants tested and the level of significance achieved. Include workings in the appendix.

Discussion

It is probably easiest to think of this as a series of subsections:

- What do your results actually show? Which hypothesis did you accept? Why? (Don't ignore any descriptive statistics: comment on these either here or next to where they are presented.)
- How do your findings fit in with the earlier research that you wrote about in the introduction? (You should not need to introduce new material here.)
- What are the limitations of your study? Were there design flaws? If you did it again how would you improve it? (Try not just to say 'More participants could have been tested'.)

- What are the implications of your findings?
- What follow-up studies can you suggest?

Conclusion

Summarise your findings in one or two sentences.

References

Include the references for:

- any names quoted in your report
- any computer packages used
- any books or journals you obtained information from

References should be in alphabetical order. To see how to present these, consult the back of any textbook. *It is easier to keep a note of references as you go along than have to go back and look them all up at the end.*

Appendices

Put everything in a logical order and make sure that everything is labelled. Appendices are looked at!

Section Sixteen

Study aids

SAMPLE EXAM QUESTIONS

Please note that marks given by the examiner in the practice essays should be used as a guide only and are not definitive.

AFB 1998 Question 12

A group of researchers wished to investigate different styles of play behaviour in infant schoolchildren. They decided to use a naturalistic observational method, based on observing and recording the play behaviour of children in their school playgrounds.

(a) Explain *two* ethical problems associated with naturalistic observational techniques which the researchers would need to take into account when planning this study. (4 marks)

(b) Explain *two* advantages that naturalistic observation would have over laboratory experimentation when studying play in young children. (4 marks)

There are obviously a lot of marks for each part of this question and it is a mistake to rush the answer.

One way in which candidates lose marks is by failing to follow the injunction 'explain'.

Candidate's answers

(a) No informed consent and hard to debrief.
   This would only get two marks. Although there is correct identification of two ethical problems, there is no explanation.

(a) The researchers should ask the children's parents for their consent and explain what the study was about to them before they began. They should also make sure that they didn't upset the children in any way while they were doing the observation.
   This would get the full four marks.

(a) There would be problems controlling variables in a naturalistic observation study.
   This would get no marks. The student didn't read the question and has not given an ethical *problem.*

(b) Naturalistic observation has more ecological validity and is cheaper.
   This would certainly get one mark, but again the student has not explained the advantages they mention.

(b) A naturalistic observation is done in the children's usual surroundings and so it has more ecological validity than a laboratory experiment. It is more likely that the findings might be true in other settings as well.

Also the children would behave naturally and not change their behaviour – in a laboratory they might do what they think the researcher wants them to do.

This would get the full four marks.

You can see that you should answer fully and be careful that you answer the question.

It is common practice to ask questions about a range of different methods. Make sure you learn the following for each of the methods mentioned on the syllabus:

- *a clear and detailed definition*
- *two advantages and two disadvantages for each method*
- *the ethical issues associated with each method*

AEB 1998 Question 13

Another common exam question describes a research study of some kind and then asks questions about it, as below.

Two students were interested in investigating participants' estimation of the duration of staged events. In a pilot investigation they had discovered that participants tend to overestimate the duration of events they witness. As a follow-up to this, they decided to investigate whether knowledge of this finding influenced such time estimations. They designed a study in which participants were randomly assigned to one of two groups, each of which witnessed a stranger enter a room. Participants in the control group were asked to estimate the length of time that the stranger was in the room (to the nearest second). Participants in the experimental group were also asked this, but these participants were also informed that people witnessing an event tend to overestimate its duration.

The results obtained for the investigation were as follows:

Participant no.	Control group (time in seconds)	Participant no.	Experimental group (time in seconds)
1	45	11	35
2	42	12	40
3	40	13	38
4	45	14	41
5	50	15	42
6	55	16	33
7	48	17	35
8	37	18	39
9	43	19	40
10	44	20	36

From the data obtained, the investigators produced the following graph:

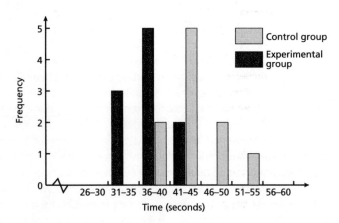

The investigators then analysed their data using an inferential statistical test. They decided to use the Mann–Whitney U-test, and found that their observed (calculated) value of $U = 9.5$. The critical (table) values of U for the appropriate sample size are:

$p = 0.01$	$p = 0.025$	$p = 0.05$
19	23	27

(a) Suggest how participants may have been randomly assigned to the two groups. (2 marks)

(b) The investigators decide to use a one-tailed (directional) hypothesis for their investigation. Suggest an appropriate one-tailed (directional) hypothesis for this study. (2 marks)

(c) State the independent and dependent variables in this study. (2 marks)

(d) Name *one* situational variable that the investigators need to control in this investigation and suggest how it might be controlled. (3 marks)

(e) Name the graphical technique used by the investigators. (1 mark)

(f) How would you interpret the data displayed on the graph? (2 marks)

(g) Suggest *two* reasons why the investigators selected the Mann–Whitney U-test to analyse the data. (2 marks)

(h) Explain why the null hypothesis for this investigation would be retained or rejected. (2 marks)

Candidate's answers

(a) A list of names could be written down in alphabetical order and the first half put in one group and the second half in the other.
This would get no marks. It is not random assignation, but systematic.

(a) Two methods could be computer selection and manual selection (names in a hat).
A partially correct answer that would get one mark – correct methods are named but exactly what would be done is not clear.

(a) Participants could be randomly assigned by putting all the names in a hat, then drawing them out: first name – Group A, second name – Group B, etc., or some similar method.
This would get both marks. A correct suggestion fully explained.

(b) Participants who are told people overestimate time will give different answers to those who don't know this.
No marks for this. The suggested hypothesis is non-directional (two-tailed).

(b) There will be a reduction in the estimates of the experimental group compared to the control group.
This would get one mark, but fails to explain what is being estimated.

(b) An experimental group who are given information regarding the overestimation of time will give lower time estimates than a group who are not given this information.
This would get two marks. Sufficiently clear and detailed for full marks.

(c) IV = estimates of time; DV = being told about overestimation.
No marks. The candidate has muddled the IV and the DV.

(c) IV = information given; DV = time.
This would get one mark for identifying the IV. However, this is a weak answer and would be an occasion when the examiner might like to give half a mark but can't!

(c) The independent variable is giving one group information about the fact time is often overestimated, and not giving it to the others. The dependent variable is the estimates of how long the stranger is in the room.
The full two marks. Clear and correct answer.

(d) They would have to make sure the stranger was always in the room for the same length of time.
One mark. Correct as far as it goes – but the student hasn't answered the second part of the question.

(d) They would have to make sure that the experimenters were not biased. This could be done by training.
No marks. This is not a situational variable.

(d) They would have to make sure that people couldn't measure the time. The experimenters would have to ask everyone for their watches and remove all clocks from the room.
Two marks. It may seem a simple answer, but it is correct!

(d) They would have to make sure that the stranger was seen by each group for the same time and behaved in the same way. This could be done by having both groups together in the same room when the stranger comes in and telling the experimental group not to tell anyone about the overestimation of time.
Two marks. Another possible correct suggestion.
There are always lots of different possible answers to this type of question, and any reasonable answer will be given credit.

(e) It is a frequency graph.
This would be awarded one mark.
There are some problems with this question and the answers 'bar chart' or 'histogram' would also have been credited. You should note that if you write down two *answers, only the first will be marked.*

(f) The experimental group are towards the low end and the control group are towards the high end.
One mark. Correct as far as it goes, but lacks detail.

(f) The experimental group times have a range from the 31–5 band to the 41–5 band whilst the control group times have a range from the 36–40 band to the 51–5 band. This suggests that the control group estimates were longer than those of the experimental group.
Two marks. A clear and detailed answer which would certainly get full marks.

(g) Because there is a repeated measures design or an independent groups design and because data is nominal/ordinal/ratio.
No marks. Contrary to what some candidates seem to believe, you can't put down every possible answer and hope to be given a mark!

(g) Because it is a test for difference and a non-parametric test.
One mark for knowing it is a test for differences.

(g) Mann–Whitney is used when there is independent groups (which there is here) and the scores collected are an ordinal level of measurement. Estimates of time would be ordinal.
Two marks. Not particularly well-phrased but this answer would get full marks.

(h) The null hypothesis would be retained.
No marks. Wrong!

(h) The null hypothesis would be rejected because the times for the experimental group were shorter than those for the control group.
One mark. A correct answer but not explained.

(h) The null hypothesis would be rejected. The observed (calculated) value of $U = 9.5$ and this is smaller than all of the critical (table) values. At $p = 0.01$ the critical value is 19. This means that there is only a 1 per cent chance that the result is due to chance so the null hypothesis would be rejected.
Two marks. A full explanation.

Appendix

Critical value tables

Table 1 Critical values of χ^2

	Level of significance for a one-tailed test					
	0.10	0.05	0.025	0.01	0.005	0.0005
	Level of significance for a two-tailed test					
df	0.20	0.10	0.05	0.02	0.01	0.001
1	1.64	2.71	3.84	5.41	6.64	10.83
2	3.22	4.60	5.99	7.82	9.21	13.82
3	4.64	6.25	7.82	9.84	11.34	16.27
4	5.99	7.78	9.49	11.67	13.28	18.46
5	7.29	9.24	11.07	13.39	15.09	20.52
6	8.56	10.64	12.59	15.03	16.81	22.46
7	9.80	12.02	14.07	16.62	18.48	24.32
8	11.03	13.36	15.51	18.17	20.09	26.12
9	12.24	14.68	16.92	19.68	21.67	27.88
10	13.44	15.99	18.31	26.16	23.21	29.59
11	14.63	17.28	19.68	22.62	24.72	31.26
12	15.81	18.55	21.03	24.05	26.22	32.91
13	16.98	19.81	22.36	25.47	27.69	34.53
14	18.15	21.06	23.68	26.87	29.14	36.12
15	19.31	22.31	25.00	28.26	30.58	37.70
16	20.46	23.54	26.30	29.63	32.00	39.29
17	21.62	24.77	27.59	31.00	33.41	40.75
18	22.76	25.99	28.87	32.35	34.80	42.31
19	23.90	27.20	30.14	33.69	36.19	43.82
20	25.04	28.41	31.41	35.02	37.57	45.32
21	26.17	29.62	32.67	36.34	38.93	46.80
22	27.30	30.81	33.92	37.66	40.29	48.27
23	28.43	32.01	35.17	38.97	41.64	49.73
24	29.55	33.20	36.42	40.27	42.98	51.18
25	30.68	34.38	37.65	41.57	44.31	52.62

	Level of significance for a one-tailed test					
	0.10	0.05	0.025	0.01	0.005	0.0005
	Level of significance for a two-tailed test					
df	0.20	0.10	0.05	0.02	0.01	0.001
26	31.80	35.56	38.88	42.86	45.64	54.05
27	32.91	36.74	40.11	44.14	46.96	55.48
28	34.03	37.92	41.34	45.42	48.28	56.89
29	35.14	39.09	42.69	49.69	49.59	58.30
30	36.25	40.26	43.77	47.96	50.89	59.70
32	38.47	42.59	46.29	50.49	53.49	62.49
34	40.68	44.90	48.60	53.00	56.06	65.25
36	42.88	47.21	51.00	55.49	58.62	67.99
38	45.08	49.51	53.38	57.97	61.16	70.70
40	47.27	51.81	55.76	60.44	63.69	73.40
44	51.64	56.37	60.48	65.34	68.71	78.75
48	55.99	60.91	65.17	70.20	73.68	84.04
52	60.33	65.42	69.83	75.02	78.62	89.27
56	64.66	69.92	74.47	79.82	83.51	94.46
60	68.97	74.40	79.08	84.58	88.38	99.61

Source: Abridged from Fisher and Yates (1974)

Note: Calculated value of χ^2 must equal or exceed the table (critical) values for significance at the level shown.

Table 2 Critical values in the binomial sign test

	Level of significance for one-tailed test				
	0.05	0.025	0.01	0.005	0.0005
	Level of significance for two-tailed test				
N	0.10	0.05	0.02	0.01	0.001
5	0	–	–	–	–
6	0	0	–	–	–
7	0	0	0	–	–
8	1	0	0	0	–
9	1	1	0	0	–
10	1	1	0	0	–
11	2	1	1	0	0
12	2	2	1	1	0
13	3	2	1	1	0
14	3	2	2	1	0
15	3	3	2	2	1
16	4	3	2	2	1
17	4	4	3	2	1
18	5	4	3	3	1
19	5	4	4	3	2
20	5	5	4	3	2
25	7	7	6	5	4
30	10	9	8	7	5
35	12	11	10	9	7

Source: From Clegg (1982). With the kind permission of the author and publishers.

Note: Calculated S must be *equal to* or *less than* the table (critical) value for significance at the level shown.

Table 3 **Critical values of *U* at various levels of probability (Mann–Whitney)**
Table 3a **Critical values of *U* for a one-tailed test at 0.005; two-tailed test at 0.01***

n_2	1	2	3	4	5	6	7	8	9	10	11	12	13	14	15	16	17	18	19	20
1	–	–	–	–	–	–	–	–	–	–	–	–	–	–	–	–	–	–	–	–
2	–	–	–	–	–	–	–	–	–	–	–	–	–	–	–	–	–	–	0	0
3	–	–	–	–	–	–	–	–	0	0	0	1	1	1	2	2	2	2	3	3
4	–	–	–	–	–	0	0	1	1	2	2	3	3	4	5	5	6	6	7	8
5	–	–	–	–	0	1	1	2	3	4	5	6	7	7	8	9	10	11	12	13
6	–	–	–	0	1	2	3	4	5	6	7	9	10	11	12	13	15	16	17	18
7	–	–	–	0	1	3	4	6	7	9	10	12	13	15	16	18	19	21	22	24
8	–	–	–	1	2	4	6	7	9	11	13	15	17	18	20	22	24	26	28	30
9	–	–	0	1	3	5	7	9	11	13	16	18	20	22	24	27	29	31	33	36
10	–	–	0	2	4	6	9	11	13	16	18	21	24	26	29	31	34	37	39	42
11	–	–	0	2	5	7	10	13	16	18	21	24	27	30	33	36	39	42	45	48
12	–	–	1	3	6	9	12	15	18	21	24	27	31	34	37	41	44	47	51	54
13	–	–	1	3	7	10	13	17	20	24	27	31	34	38	42	45	49	53	56	60
14	–	–	1	4	7	11	15	18	22	26	30	34	38	42	46	50	54	58	63	67
15	–	–	2	5	8	12	16	20	24	29	33	37	42	46	51	55	60	64	69	73
16	–	–	2	5	9	13	18	22	27	31	36	41	45	50	55	60	65	70	74	79
17	–	–	2	6	10	15	19	24	29	34	39	44	49	54	60	65	70	75	81	86
18	–	–	2	6	11	16	21	26	31	37	42	47	53	58	64	70	75	81	87	92
19	–	0	3	7	12	17	22	28	33	39	45	51	56	63	69	74	81	87	93	99
20	–	0	3	8	13	18	24	30	36	42	48	54	60	67	73	79	86	92	99	105

* Dashes in the body of the table indicate that no decision is possible at the stated level of significance.

Note: For any n_1 and n_2 the observed value of *U* is significant at a given level of significance if it is *equal to* or *less than* the critical values shown in tables 3(a)–(d).

Table 3b Critical values of U for a one-tailed test at 0.01; two-tailed test at 0.02*

	n_1																			
n_2	1	2	3	4	5	6	7	8	9	10	11	12	13	14	15	16	17	18	19	20
1	–	–	–	–	–	–	–	–	–	–	–	–	–	–	–	–	–	–	–	–
2	–	–	–	–	–	–	–	–	–	–	–	–	0	0	0	0	0	0	1	1
3	–	–	–	–	–	–	0	0	1	1	1	2	2	2	3	3	4	4	4	5
4	–	–	–	–	0	1	1	2	3	3	4	5	5	6	7	7	8	9	9	10
5	–	–	–	0	1	2	3	4	5	6	7	8	9	10	11	12	13	14	15	16
6	–	–	–	1	2	3	4	6	7	8	9	11	12	13	15	16	18	19	20	22
7	–	–	0	1	3	4	6	7	9	11	12	14	16	17	19	21	23	24	26	28
8	–	–	0	2	4	6	7	9	11	13	15	17	20	22	24	26	28	30	32	34
9	–	–	1	3	5	7	9	11	14	16	18	21	23	26	28	31	33	36	38	40
10	–	–	1	3	6	8	11	13	16	19	22	24	27	30	33	36	38	41	44	47
11	–	–	1	4	7	9	12	15	18	22	25	28	31	34	37	41	44	47	50	53
12	–	–	2	5	8	11	14	17	21	24	28	31	35	38	42	46	49	53	56	60
13	–	0	2	5	9	12	16	20	23	27	31	35	39	43	47	51	55	59	63	67
14	–	0	2	6	10	13	17	22	26	30	34	38	43	47	51	56	60	65	69	73
15	–	0	3	7	11	15	19	24	28	33	37	42	47	51	56	61	66	70	75	80
16	–	0	3	7	12	16	21	26	31	36	41	46	51	56	61	66	71	76	82	87
17	–	0	4	8	13	18	23	28	33	38	44	49	55	60	66	71	77	82	88	93
18	–	0	4	9	14	19	24	30	36	41	47	53	59	65	70	76	82	88	94	100
19	–	1	4	9	15	20	26	32	38	44	50	56	63	69	75	82	88	94	101	107
20	–	1	5	10	16	22	28	34	40	47	53	60	67	73	80	87	93	100	107	114

* Dashes in the body of the table indicate that no decision is possible at the stated level of significance.

Table 3c Critical values of *U* for a one-tailed test at 0.025; two-tailed test at 0.05*

n_2	1	2	3	4	5	6	7	8	9	10	11	12	13	14	15	16	17	18	19	20
																		n_1		
1	–	–	–	–	–	–	–	–	–	–	–	–	–	–	–	–	–	–	–	–
2	–	–	–	–	–	–	–	0	0	0	0	1	1	1	1	1	2	2	2	2
3	–	–	–	–	0	1	1	2	2	3	3	4	4	5	5	6	6	7	7	8
4	–	–	–	0	1	2	3	4	4	5	6	7	8	9	10	11	11	12	13	13
5	–	–	0	1	2	3	5	6	7	8	9	11	12	13	14	15	17	18	19	20
6	–	–	1	2	3	5	6	8	10	11	13	14	16	17	19	21	22	24	25	27
7	–	–	1	3	5	6	8	10	12	14	16	18	20	22	24	26	28	30	32	34
8	–	0	2	4	6	8	10	13	15	17	19	22	24	26	29	31	34	36	38	41
9	–	0	2	4	7	10	12	15	17	20	23	26	28	31	34	37	39	42	45	48
10	–	0	3	5	8	11	14	17	20	23	26	29	33	36	39	42	45	48	52	55
11	–	0	3	6	9	13	16	19	23	26	30	33	37	40	44	47	51	55	58	62
12	–	1	4	7	11	14	18	22	26	29	33	37	41	45	49	53	57	61	65	69
13	–	1	4	8	12	16	20	24	28	33	37	41	45	50	54	59	63	67	72	76
14	–	1	5	9	13	17	22	26	31	36	40	45	50	55	59	64	67	74	78	83
15	–	1	5	10	14	19	24	29	34	39	44	49	54	59	64	70	75	80	85	90
16	–	1	6	11	15	21	26	31	37	42	47	53	59	64	70	75	81	86	92	98
17	–	2	6	11	17	22	28	34	39	45	51	57	63	67	75	81	87	93	99	105
18	–	2	7	12	18	24	30	36	42	48	55	61	67	74	80	86	93	99	106	112
19	–	2	7	13	19	25	32	38	45	52	58	65	72	78	85	92	99	106	113	119
20	–	2	8	13	20	27	34	41	48	55	62	69	76	83	90	98	105	112	119	127

* Dashes in the body of the table indicate that no decision is possible at the stated level of significance.

Table 3d Critical values of U for a one-tailed test at 0.05; two-tailed test at 0.10[*]

n_2 \ n_1	1	2	3	4	5	6	7	8	9	10	11	12	13	14	15	16	17	18	19	20
1	–	–	–	–	–	–	–	–	–	–	–	–	–	–	–	–	–	–	0	0
2	–	–	–	–	0	0	0	1	1	1	1	2	2	2	3	3	3	4	4	4
3	–	–	0	0	1	2	2	3	3	4	5	5	6	7	7	8	9	9	10	11
4	–	–	0	1	2	3	4	5	6	7	8	9	10	11	12	14	15	16	17	18
5	–	0	1	2	4	5	6	8	9	11	12	13	15	16	18	19	20	22	23	25
6	–	0	2	3	5	7	8	10	12	14	16	17	19	21	23	25	26	28	30	32
7	–	0	2	4	6	8	11	13	15	17	19	21	24	26	28	30	33	35	37	39
8	–	1	3	5	8	10	13	15	18	20	23	26	28	31	33	36	39	41	44	47
9	–	1	3	6	9	12	15	18	21	24	27	30	33	36	39	42	45	48	51	54
10	–	1	4	7	11	14	17	20	24	27	31	34	37	41	44	48	51	55	58	62
11	–	1	5	8	12	16	19	23	27	31	34	38	42	46	50	54	57	61	65	69
12	–	2	5	9	13	17	21	26	30	34	38	42	47	51	55	60	64	68	72	77
13	–	2	6	10	15	19	24	28	33	37	42	47	51	56	61	65	70	75	80	84
14	–	2	7	11	16	21	26	31	36	41	46	51	56	61	66	71	77	82	87	92
15	–	3	7	12	18	23	28	33	39	44	50	55	61	66	72	77	83	88	94	100
16	–	3	8	14	19	25	30	36	42	48	54	60	65	71	77	83	89	95	101	107
17	–	3	9	15	20	26	33	39	45	51	57	64	70	77	83	89	96	102	109	115
18	–	4	9	16	22	28	35	41	48	55	61	68	75	82	88	95	102	109	116	123
19	0	4	10	17	23	30	37	44	51	58	65	72	80	87	94	101	109	116	123	130
20	0	4	11	18	25	32	39	47	54	62	69	77	84	92	100	107	115	123	130	138

* Dashes in the body of the table indicate that no decision is possible at the stated level of significance.

Table 4 Critical values of W at various levels of probability (Wilcoxon)*

	Level of significance for one-tailed test					Level of significance for one-tailed test			
	0.05	0.025	0.01	0.005		0.05	0.025	0.01	0.005
	Level of significance for two-tailed test					Level of significance for two-tailed test			
N	0.10	0.05	0.02	0.01	N	0.10	0.05	0.02	0.01
5	1	–	–	–	28	130	117	102	92
6	2	1	–	–	29	141	127	111	100
7	4	2	0	–	30	152	137	120	109
8	6	4	2	0	31	163	148	130	118
9	8	6	3	2	32	175	159	141	128
10	11	8	5	3	33	188	171	151	138
11	14	11	7	5	34	201	183	162	149
12	17	14	10	7	35	214	195	174	160
13	21	17	13	10	36	228	208	186	171
14	26	21	16	13	37	242	222	198	183
15	30	25	20	16	38	256	235	211	195
16	36	30	24	19	39	271	250	224	208
17	41	35	28	23	40	287	264	238	221
18	47	40	33	28	41	303	279	252	234
19	54	46	38	32	42	319	295	267	248
20	60	52	43	37	43	336	311	281	262
21	68	59	49	43	44	353	327	297	277
22	75	66	56	49	45	371	344	313	292
23	83	73	62	55	46	389	361	329	307
24	92	81	69	61	47	408	379	345	323
25	101	90	77	68	48	427	397	362	339
26	110	98	85	76	49	446	415	380	356
27	120	107	93	84	50	466	434	398	373

* Dashes in the table indicate that no decision is possible at the stated level of significance.

Note The statistic W denotes the smaller sum of ranks associated with differences that are all of the same sign. For any N (number of subjects or pairs of matched subjects) the observed value of W is significant at a given level of significance if it is *equal to* or *less than* the critical values shown in the table.

Table 5 Critical values of *t* at various levels of probability (*t*-test)

df	Level of significance for one-tailed test					
	0.10	0.05	0.025	0.01	0.005	0.0005
	Level of significance for two-tailed test					
	0.20	0.10	0.05	0.02	0.01	0.001
1	3.078	6.314	12.706	31.821	63.657	636.619
2	1.886	2.920	4.303	6.965	9.925	31.598
3	1.638	2.353	3.182	4.541	5.841	12.941
4	1.533	2.132	2.776	3.747	4.604	8.610
5	1.476	2.015	2.571	3.365	4.032	6.859
6	1.440	1.943	2.447	3.143	3.707	5.959
7	1.415	1.895	2.365	2.998	3.499	5.405
8	1.397	1.860	2.306	2.896	3.355	5.041
9	1.383	1.833	2.262	2.821	3.250	4.781
10	1.372	1.812	2.228	2.764	3.169	4.587
11	1.363	1.796	2.201	2.718	3.106	4.437
12	1.356	1.782	2.179	2.681	3.055	4.318
13	1.350	1.771	2.160	2.650	3.012	4.221
14	1.345	1.761	2.145	2.624	2.977	4.140
15	1.341	1.753	2.131	2.602	2.947	4.073
16	1.337	1.746	2.120	2.583	2.921	4.015
17	1.333	1.740	2.110	2.567	2.898	3.965
18	1.330	1.734	2.101	2.552	2.878	3.922
19	1.328	1.729	2.093	2.539	2.861	3.883
20	1.325	1.725	2.086	2.528	2.845	3.850
21	1.323	1.721	2.080	2.518	2.831	3.819
22	1.321	1.717	2.074	2.508	2.819	3.792
23	1.319	1.714	2.069	2.500	2.807	3.767
24	1.318	1.711	2.064	2.492	2.797	3.745
25	1.316	1.708	2.060	2.485	2.787	3.725

	\multicolumn{6}{c|}{Level of significance for one-tailed test}					
	0.10	0.05	0.025	0.01	0.005	0.0005
	\multicolumn{6}{c}{Level of significance for two-tailed test}					
df	0.20	0.10	0.05	0.02	0.01	0.001
26	1.315	1.706	2.056	2.497	2.779	3.707
27	1.314	1.703	2.052	2.473	2.771	3.690
28	1.313	1.701	2.048	2.467	2.763	3.674
29	1.311	1.699	2.045	2.462	2.756	3.659
30	1.310	1.697	2.042	2.457	2.750	3.646
40	1.303	1.684	2.021	2.423	2.704	3.551
60	1.296	1.671	2.000	2.390	2.660	3.460
120	1.289	1.658	1.980	2.358	2.617	3.373
∞	1.282	1.645	1.960	2.326	2.576	3.291

Note 1 For any particular *df* the observed value of *t* is significant at a given level of significance if it is *equal to* or *larger than* the critical values shown in the table.

Note 2 When there is no exact *df* use the next lowest number, except for very large *df*s (well over 120), when you can use the infinity (∞) row.

Table 6 Critical values of Spearman's r_S			
	Level of significance for a two-tailed test		
	0.10	0.05	0.02	0.01
	Level of significance for a one-tailed test		
n	0.05	0.025	0.01	0.005
4	1.000	–	–	–
5	0.900	1.000	1.000	–
6	0.829	0.886	0.943	1.000
7	0.714	0.786	0.893	0.929
8	0.643	0.738	0.833	0.881
9	0.600	0.700	0.783	0.833
10	0.564	0.648	0.745	0.794
11	0.536	0.618	0.709	0.755
12	0.503	0.587	0.671	0.727
13	0.484	0.560	0.648	0.703
14	0.464	0.538	0.622	0.675
15	0.443	0.521	0.604	0.654
16	0.429	0.503	0.582	0.635
17	0.414	0.485	0.566	0.615
18	0.401	0.472	0.550	0.600
19	0.391	0.460	0.535	0.584
20	0.380	0.447	0.520	0.570
21	0.370	0.435	0.508	0.556
22	0.361	0.425	0.496	0.544
23	0.353	0.415	0.486	0.532
24	0.344	0.406	0.476	0.521
25	0.337	0.398	0.466	0.511
26	0.331	0.390	0.457	0.501
27	0.324	0.382	0.448	0.491
28	0.317	0.375	0.440	0.483
29	0.312	0.368	0.433	0.475
30	0.306	0.362	0.425	0.467

Table 6 continued

Note: For $n > 30$, the significance of r_s can be tested by using the formula:

$$t = r_s \sqrt{\frac{n-2}{1-r_s^2}} \qquad df = n-2$$

and checking the value of t in Table 7.

Calculated r_s must *equal* or *exceed* the table (critical) value for significance at the level shown.

Table 7 Critical values of t

	Level of significance for a one-tailed test			
	0.05	0.025	0.01	0.005
	Level of significance for a two-tailed test			
df	0.10	0.05	0.02	0.01
1	6.314	12.706	31.821	63.657
2	2.920	4.303	6.965	9.925
3	2.353	3.182	4.541	5.841
4	2.132	2.776	3.747	4.604
5	2.015	2.571	3.365	4.032
6	1.943	2.447	3.143	3.707
7	1.895	2.365	2.998	3.499
8	1.860	2.306	2.896	3.355
9	1.833	2.262	2.821	3.250
10	1.812	2.228	2.764	3.169
11	1.796	2.201	2.718	3.106
12	1.782	2.179	2.681	3.055
13	1.771	2.160	2.650	3.012
14	1.761	2.145	2.624	2.977
15	1.753	2.131	2.602	2.947
16	1.746	2.120	2.583	2.921
17	1.740	2.110	2.567	2.898
18	1.734	2.101	2.552	2.878
19	1.729	2.093	2.539	2.861
20	1.725	2.086	2.528	2.845
21	1.721	2.080	2.518	2.831
22	1.717	2.074	2.508	2.819
23	1.714	2.069	2.500	2.807
24	1.711	2.064	2.492	2.797
25	1.708	2.060	2.485	2.787
26	1.706	2.056	2.479	2.779
27	1.703	2.052	2.473	2.771
28	1.701	2.048	2.467	2.763

	Level of significance for a one-tailed test			
	0.05	0.025	0.01	0.005
	Level of significance for a two-tailed test			
df	0.10	0.05	0.02	0.01
29	1.699	2.045	2.462	2.756
30	1.697	2.042	2.457	2.750
40	1.684	2.021	2.423	2.704
60	1.671	2.000	2.390	2.660
120	1.658	1.980	2.358	2.617
∞	1.645	1.960	2.326	2.576

Source: Abridged from Fisher and Yates (1974)

Note: Calculated *t* must *equal* or *exceed* the table (critical) value for significance at the level shown.

Table 8 Critical values of Pearson's *r*			
	Level of significance for a one-tailed test		
	0.05	0.025	0.005	0.0005
df	Level of significance for a two-tailed test		
(N − 2)	0.10	0.05	0.01	0.001
2	0.9000	0.9500	0.9900	0.9999
3	0.805	0.878	0.9587	0.9911
4	0.729	0.811	0.9172	0.9741
5	0.669	0.754	0.875	0.9509
6	0.621	0.707	0.834	0.9241
7	0.582	0.666	0.798	0.898
8	0.549	0.632	0.765	0.872
9	0.521	0.602	0.735	0.847
10	0.497	0.576	0.708	0.823
11	0.476	0.553	0.684	0.801
12	0.475	0.532	0.661	0.780
13	0.441	0.514	0.641	0.760
14	0.426	0.497	0.623	0.742
15	0.412	0.482	0.606	0.725
16	0.400	0.468	0.590	0.708
17	0.389	0.456	0.575	0.693
18	0.378	0.444	0.561	0.679
19	0.369	0.433	0.549	0.665
20	0.360	0.423	0.537	0.652
25	0.323	0.381	0.487	0.597
30	0.296	0.349	0.449	0.554
35	0.275	0.325	0.418	0.519
40	0.257	0.304	0.393	0.490
45	0.243	0.288	0.372	0.465
50	0.231	0.273	0.354	0.443
60	0.211	0.250	0.325	0.408
70	0.195	0.232	0.302	0.380
80	0.183	0.217	0.283	0.357

	Level of significance for a one-tailed test			
	0.05	0.025	0.005	0.0005
df	Level of significance for a two-tailed test			
(N − 2)	0.10	0.05	0.01	0.001
90	0.173	0.205	0.267	0.338
100	0.164	0.195	0.254	0.321

Source From Powell (1976). With kind permission of the author and publishers.

Note Calculated *r* must *equal* or *exceed* the table (critical) value for significance at the level shown.

Glossary

The first occurrence of each of these terms is highlighted in **bold** type in the main text.

alternative hypothesis The converse of the null hypothesis. A fully operationalised hypothesis which states that there is a difference/correlation between the measures obtained.

average A measure of what is a typical value in a set of scores. (Often used in a mathematical sense as the *mean*.)

between groups/subjects/participants design *See* independent groups /measures design.

biased sample A sample selected from the population in such a way that some people have a greater chance of being picked than others.

bimodal distribution A frequency distribution where there are two modes.

case study A detailed study of one individual or a small group.

ceiling effect This occurs when the test being used does not discriminate between participants because it is too easy for them and they all get very high scores.

central tendency Descriptive statistics indicating the mid-point of a set of scores (*mean, median* or *mode*).

clinical interview *See* semi-structured interview.

clinical study Usually a case study conducted in connection with therapy.

cohort study A study which compares groups of participants born in different years – e.g. twenty people born in 1950, twenty born in 1960 and twenty born in 1970 – and follows each group for a number of years. Thus if the study in question began in 1980 and lasted for ten years, it would follow twenty people from the ages of ten to twenty, twenty people from twenty to thirty and twenty people from thirty to forty. The age span ten to forty years is therefore covered in only ten years.

concordance rate This indicates the closeness of the agreement or relationship between two things. If there is a perfect match between them (e.g. eye colour in identical twins), the concordance rate is 1.00. If the match is not as close the concordance rate will be lower.

concurrent validity A measure of the extent to which a test result (e.g. IQ score) is a good match with some other current indicator with which it would be expected to be related (e.g. academic performance).

confounding variable A factor which is not controlled in an experiment and which affects the behaviour being studied (the dependent variable). For example changes in noise levels due to roadworks outside the test room might affect memory scores. This means that it is impossible to conclude that changes which occur are due to the changes made by the researcher to the independent variable – they could be due to the influence of this confounding variable.

constructivism The idea that the meaning of an event is constructed by the individual in the light of their own experiences, i.e. it is affected by cultural and historical differences.

content analysis The analysis of something people have produced, such as a film, speech, letter and so on. Individuals are studied indirectly by a detailed analysis of such material, e.g. changes in gender stereotypes might be studied by analysing how the content of children's reading books has changed over forty years.

content validity If a test has good content validity, the questions it contains cover the whole spread of the relevant topic area.

continuous measurement Measurement of characteristics (such as height, speed of reaction, etc.) that are measured on continuous scales capable of subdivisions.

control group A group which does not receive the treatment being tested. Used as a comparison to the experimental group to study any effects of the treatment.

correlation A measure of the extent to which two variables are related.

correlation coefficient A number which indicates the strength of a correlation from -1.00 (perfect negative correlation) through 0 (no relationship) to $+1.00$ (perfect positive correlation).

counterbalancing A technique which alters the order of conditions so as to control for order effects. Some participants do task A then B, some do task B then A.

cross-cultural study A comparison of two or more cultures (such as England and France) which looks at how people are affected by the different experiences they undergo in each culture.

cross-sectional research Comparing samples of different age groups at a particular point in time (e.g. children aged four, eight and twelve in 1998).

debriefing Explaining the details of an investigation to participants after they have taken part in it. Participants should leave the research in the same state as they entered it.

deception The deliberate misleading of participants during an investigation. Deception means that participants have not given *informed consent* before they take part in research.

demand characteristics Participants will try to guess what is the purpose of any research and what the researcher is hoping they will do. Demand characteristics are the clues participants may pick up as to what the research is about.

dependent variable The variable which the researcher measures.

descriptive statistics Methods of organising and summarising data – such as graphs, *means*, *range*, and so on.

deviation The difference between an individual score and the mean of the set of scores that includes it.

directional hypothesis A hypothesis which predicts a difference or a correlation between two variables and which predicts the direction of that difference or correlation.

discourse analysis A technique which attempts to analyse the meaning behind the words we use in communication and the way in which we use them. For example: do we talk of 'ethnic cleansing' or 'extermination'? *How* do we speak? hesitantly? confidently? and so on.

discrete measurement Measurement of something with discrete categories (being born in England/Scotland/Wales; studying history/not studying history).

dispersion The 'spread-outness' of a set of scores.

distribution-free statistical tests Also called *non-parametric tests*. A type of inferential statistical test which does not make underlying mathematical assumptions about the distribution of scores in the population being studied (e.g. Mann–Whitney U-test or Spearman's rho).

double blind procedure A technique where neither the researcher nor the participant knows who is in each treatment condition. For example, in a test of a new drug half the participants receive the drug and half a placebo. The participants do not know who has received the drug and neither do the researchers handing out the pills and measuring their effects.

ecological validity The degree to which the findings of the research can be generalised to other settings other than the one in which the research was conducted.

empirical Derived from observation or experiments.

event sampling A technique used in an observational study whereby a record is made every time a certain event occurs.

experiment A method involving the manipulation of one variable (the *independent variable*) by the researcher and the measurement of any effects on another variable (the *dependent variable*). In addition purists argue that in a true experiment it is possible to allocate any participant to any condition.

experimental designs *See* separate entries on *repeated measures design, matched pairs design, independent groups design* and *single participant design*.

experimental group The group of participants for whom the independent variable is altered.

experimenter bias This occurs if the researcher's expectations affect the results of the study.

external validity External validity measures the extent to which the results can be applied to other situations, to the future, and so on. Also known as *population validity*.

face validity Whether a test looks as though it is measuring what it is meant to measure.

field experiment An experiment conducted in a natural setting rather than in a laboratory.

field research/study Research conducted in a natural setting.

floor effect This occurs when the test being used does not discriminate between participants because it is too difficult for them and they all get very low scores.

generalisability The issue as to whether it can be assumed that a result can be applied to situations or groups of people other than those used in the original research.

hypothesis A testable statement made at the beginning of an investigation which the researcher aims to support or refute.

idiographic approach An approach concerned with the behaviour of each unique individual rather than trying to establish general laws of behaviour which apply to all.

independent groups/measures design An experimental design where each participant is tested in only one condition. Also called a *between groups/subjects/participants design*.

independent variable The variable which the researcher manipulates.

informed consent An ethical consideration regarding participants in an experiment: do they fully understand what will happen during the research before they agree to take part?

inter-judge/inter-observer/inter-rater reliability The degree to which the measurements obtained by two observers or judges agree or correlate.

internal validity Internal validity is concerned with whether the results obtained are really produced by the manipulation of the independent variable.

interval level of measurement A scale with equal units of measurement throughout the scale but without a true zero (e.g. temperature).

levels of measurement This refers to the way in which data is measured. The different levels – *nominal, ordinal, interval* and *ratio* – give different types of information about the data collected (see separate glossary entries).

longitudinal study A method whereby participants are studied over a number of years (e.g. from birth to eleven years old).

matched pairs design An experimental design in which participants in each condition are matched on variables which are thought important to the results of that particular study (e.g. age, IQ, class etc.).

mean A measure of *central tendency*. The sum of the scores divided by the number of scores.

measure of dispersion A measure of the 'spread-outness' of a set of scores (e.g. *range* and *standard deviation*).

median A measure of *central tendency*. The middle of a set of scores.

mode A measure of *central tendency*. The most frequent score.

multimodal A sample which has more than one mode. If there are two modes the sample is said to be *bimodal* (e.g. 2 2 2 4 6 7 7 7); if there are more than two modes it is said to be multimodal (e.g. 1 1 1 3 4 4 4 6 8 8 8).

natural experiment An experiment in which the independent variable alters because of naturally occurring factors – not because of manipulation by the researcher.

naturalistic observation Unobtrusively observing behaviour in a natural setting. The investigator does nothing to interfere with the behaviour being observed.

negative correlation A relationship between two variables where, as one increases, the other decreases.

nominal level of measurement The data merely indicates the numbers falling into the various categories collected (such as blonde/brunette/redhead; male/female; over twenty-one/under twenty-one, etc.).

nomothetic approach A method or approach which seeks to establish general laws of behaviour.

non-directional hypothesis A hypothesis which predicts a difference or correlation between two variables but which does not predict the direction of the difference or correlation.

non-directive interview *See* unstructured interview.

non-parametric test Also called a *distribution-free test* because assumptions are not made about the distribution of scores in the population. Such tests can be used with skewed distributions and with data at the *ordinal* or *nominal* level.

normal distribution curve A bell-shaped distribution curve where the *mean*, *median* and *mode* are the same.

null hypothesis The hypothesis based on the statistical assumption that the scores obtained are drawn from the same population. The null hypothesis accounts for the observed results by attributing them to chance.

objective The truth or falsehood of something can be demonstrated convincingly to others. (Contrast with *subjective*.)

observer bias A tendency among observers for them to see what they expect to happen rather than to objectively record what actually happens.

one-tailed test A test used in the analysis of data when the researcher has predicted the direction of the expected result. (Also called a *directional test*.)

operationalise Usually used in a phrase such as 'operationalise the variables'. An operational definition is one which precisely defines the terms being used. Thus to operationalise variables means to define them in such a way that they can be measured.

opportunity sampling A method of sampling which takes advantage of whoever is available at a particular time at a particular location.

order effect Participants' performance in the conditions of an experiment may vary just because of the order in which they do them. They may be tired or bored after condition one and so do worse on condition two – or alternatively the practice of condition one may aid the performance of condition two.

ordinal level of measurement A measurement scale which enables us to rank scores in order.

parametric test An inferential statistical test based on mathematics which assume that certain 'parameters' are met in the population under study and in the set of scores. These parameters are that there is similar *variance* in the sets of scores, that the data is at least at interval level, and that there is a roughly normal distribution of the variable in the population from which the scores are drawn.

participant observation An observational technique in which the observer joins the group which is being observed and actively participates in group activities.

pilot study A small-scale version of a study conducted before the main research.

population The group of people who are under study and to whom the results of the research will apply.

positive correlation A relationship between two variables such that as one increases so does the other.

power The power of a statistical test indicates its ability to indicate whether the null hypothesis can be rejected when it is false.

practice effect An improvement in performance because the person has done the test before.

predictive validity If the results of a test are good predictors of that person's future performance then the test is said to have good predictive validity.

probability A number (between 0 and 1) which expresses how likely it is that an event will occur. A probability of 1 indicates the event is certain to occur. The nearer the probability is to 0 the less likely it is that the event will occur.

qualitative research Research which concentrates on the *'quality'* of the data collected – feelings, emotions, how things are expressed, and so on – rather than 'number crunching'.

quantitative data Data concerned with how *much* there is of something, how fast things are done, and so on. The data collected will be in the form of numbers.

quasi-experiment An experiment where the researcher does not allocate participants to the different conditions but takes advantage of divisions that exist naturally (e.g. age, gender, etc.).

quota sampling The participants are selected so that the sample matches the total population as regards the percentage representation of each group within it. For example if you were conducting a study in which nationality was important and if 10 per cent of the total population being studied is French, 15 per cent Spanish, 30 per cent Swiss, etc., then the representation of different nationalities selected for the sample should be in the same proportions.

random sampling A method of sampling whereby every individual in the population being studied has an equal chance of being selected.

range A measure of the spread of scores from the highest to the lowest.

ranks Putting a list of scores in order of size and then allocating Rank 1 to the smallest, Rank 2 to the next, and so on. Ranks are commonly used instead of the actual measurements taken when using an *ordinal* scale.

ratio level of measurement The level of measurement where each interval on the scale is of equal size and where the lowest point of the scale is zero. Examples are time measured in seconds and weight measured in grams.

reliability The consistency with which a result is obtained.

repeated measures design Several measures are taken from the same participant.

research hypothesis A hypothesis put forward at the beginning of a study which predicts what is expected to happen in that particular investigation.

response set A tendency to reply in the same way to items in a test, e.g. always to answer 'Yes' in a questionnaire.

retrospective study The researcher works backwards from the present day collecting information about what happened to the participant in earlier years.

robust A statistical test is said to be robust when it gives satisfactory estimates of probability, even when the data collected falls somewhat short of meeting the underlying parameters for the test.

sample A subset of the population.

sampling The process by which the researcher selects a subset of individuals from the population. Common methods in psychology include *opportunity sampling*, *random sampling* and *stratified sampling* (see individual glossary entries).

scattergram A graphical representation of the correlation between two sets of scores.

scientific method The use of methods that are objective and repeatable. Hypotheses are derived from objective observations or earlier research, the studies are well-designed (controlling for the possible influence of extraneous factors), gather data systematically and accurately, and can be replicated.

self-selected/volunteer sample The participants select themselves – e.g. by choosing to fill in a questionnaire in a newspaper.

semi-interquartile range Half of the range between the values which cut off the top and bottom 25 per cent of a set of scores, i.e. the range from the top of the first quartile to the bottom of the fourth quartile. In a list of scores such as 1 2 2/4 5 5/6 6 6/7 8 9, 2 is the top of the first quartile, 7 is the bottom of the top quartile and the distance between these scores is 5, so the semi-interquartile range is 2.5.

semi-structured (informal) interview An interview method using flexible questions to find out how a person feels about something.

significance level An indication (usually expressed as 0.05, 0.01, etc.) of the probability of obtaining the results collected if the *null hypothesis* is true. If the significance level is 0.05 or less, it is conventional to reject the null hypothesis and accept the *alternative hypothesis* – that there is a difference (or *correlation*) between the sets of data collected.

significance test A test which calculates the probability of obtaining the scores collected if the *null hypothesis* is true (i.e. if the scores are actually from the same population of scores).

single blind procedure An experimental procedure in which the participants do not know the *research hypothesis* (i.e. what is being investigated).

single participant/subject design A design where there is only one participant used in an experiment.

skewed distribution The distribution of scores is not symmetrical (as in a *normal distribution*) but the scores are concentrated towards one end or the other.

snowball sample If it is difficult to find suitable participants (e.g. if you were investigating an illegal activity), you might begin with one person and ask them if they know of other people who fit the criteria. Thus the sample 'snowballs'.

standard deviation A measure of the spread of scores. The standard deviation is calculated from the *dispersion* of scores around the *mean*.

standard score A measure of the deviation of an individual score expressed in terms of the number of standard deviations that score is from the mean (i.e. a standard score of $+1.5$ indicates a score is one-and-a-half standard deviations above the mean). Also known as a *z-score*.

standardisation This word is used in two ways: *standardised procedures* or *instructions* mean that each participant has the same experience in the research because the same things are done or said to them;

the term is also used to describe the process by which a psychological test is given to a large number of the population so that it is possible to draw up tables of the scores commonly obtained by people.

stem and leaf diagram A way of tabulating data which is a useful indicator of the distribution of scores.

stratified sample The sample is selected from the population so that relevant groups in that population are represented in the same proportions. For example if 60 per cent of the population is male then 60 per cent of the sample will be male too.

structured (formal) interview An interview in which there is a set of questions that are always asked in the same order.

subjective Based on the opinions, preferences, etc. of the individual.

systematic sampling A sample is selected from the total population in some systematic way – such as picking every fifth name from a school register, visiting every tenth house in a street, and so on.

test validity This refers to whether a test is measuring what it is supposed to measure.

time sampling A technique used in an observational study whereby a participant is studied for brief periods – e.g. for thirty seconds every five minutes (*time interval sampling*) or at a fixed point every five minutes (*time point sampling*).

two-tailed hypothesis Now more correctly referred to as a *non-directional hypothesis*. Predicts there will be a difference or a correlation but does not predict the direction of the difference.

two-tailed test A statistical test used when the hypothesis does not predict the direction of the results.

Type I error Concluding that the null hypothesis is false when in fact it is true.

Type II error Failing to reject the null hypothesis when in fact there is a good chance that it is false.

unfalsifiable If a hypothesis cannot be disproved by data then it is *unfalsifiable*. This means it lacks any scientific value, for if something cannot be disproved, then it is not possible to prove it true either.

unstructured interview Instead of having a list of scripted questions the interviewer asks questions spontaneously.

validity Validity refers to whether a test or measure is actually measuring what it is supposed to measure. *See* separate entries on *internal validity*, *external validity* and *test validity*.

variable Any thing which can change (or vary) in an investigation.

variance A measure of the *dispersion* of scores. (It is the square of the *standard deviation*.)

within subjects/participants design Another name for a *repeated measures design*.

z-score *See* standard score.

Bibliography

Ainsworth, M.D.S., Bell, S.M.V. and Stayton, D.J. (1971) 'Individual differences in the strange situation behaviour of one-year-olds', in H.R. Schaffer (ed.) *The Origins of Human Social Relations*, New York: Academic Press.

Asch, S.E. (1955) 'Opinions and social pressure', *Scientific American* 193 (5): 31–5.

Bandura, A., Ross, D. and Ross, S.A. (1963) 'Imitation of film-mediated aggressive models', *Journal of Abnormal and Social Psychology* 66: 3–11.

Barber, T.X. (1976) *Pitfalls in Human Research*, Oxford: Pergamon.

Baron, R.A. (1977) *Human Aggression*, New York: Plenum Press.

Bartlett, F.C. (1932) *Remembering*, Cambridge: Cambridge University Press.

Berry, J.W., Poortinga, Y.H., Segall, M.H. and Dasen, P.R. (1992) *Cross-cultural Psychology: Research and Applications*, New York: Cambridge University Press.

Bracht, G.H. and Glass, G.V. (1968) 'The external validity of experiments', *American Education Research Journal* 5: 437–74.

Brown, R. (1973) *A First Language: The Early Stages*, Cambridge, MA: Harvard University Press.

Burt, C.L. (1958) 'The intelligence of mental ability', *American Psychologist* 13: 1–15.

Cardwell, M.C. (1996) *The Complete A–Z of Psychology Handbook*, London: Hodder and Stoughton.

Cardwell, M.C., Clark, L. and Meldrum, C. (1996) *Psychology for A-level*, London: Harper Collins.

Clegg, F. (1982) *Simple Statistics*, Cambridge: Cambridge University Press.

Cochran, W.G. (1954) 'Some methods for strengthening common chi-square tests', *Biometrics* 10: 417–51.

Coolican, H. (1994) *Research Methods and Statistics in Psychology*, London: Hodder and Stoughton.

Dellerba, M. and Hodges, S. (1998) Unpublished coursework.

Ebbinghaus, H. (1885) *On Memory*, Leipzig: Duncker.

Eron, L.D., Huesmann, L.R., Brice, P., Fischer, P. and Mermelstein, R. (1983) 'Age trends in the development of aggression, sex-typing and related television habits', *Developmental Psychology* 19: 71–7.

Festinger, L., Schachter, S. and Back, K. (1950) *Social Pressures in Informal Groups*, New York: Harper Collins.

Fisher, R.A. and Yates, F. (1974) *Statistical Tables for Biological, Agricultural and Medical Research*, 6th edn, London: Longman.

Gardner, B.T. and Gardner, R.A. (1969) 'Teaching sign language to a chimp', *Science* 165: 664–72.

Gilligan, C. (1982) *In a Different Voice: Psychological Theory and Women's Development*, Cambridge, MA: Harvard University Press.

Goodall, J. (1978) 'Chimp killings: Is it the man in them?', *Science News* 165: 276.

Graebner, D.B. (1972) 'A decade of sexism in readers', *Reader Teacher* 26 (1): 52–8.

Griffin, C. (1985) *Typical Girls: Young Women from School to the Job Market*, London and New York: Routledge.

—— (1991) 'Experiencing power: Dimensions of gender, "race" and class', paper presented at BPS/WIPS Women and Psychology Conference, Edinburgh University, July.

—— (1995) 'Feminism, social psychology and qualitative research', *The Psychologist* 8 (3): 119–22.

Haney, C., Banks, W.C. and Zimbardo, P.G. (1973) 'A study of prisoners and guards in a simulated prison', *Naval Research Review* 30: 4–17.

Hughes, M. (1975) 'Egocentrism in preschool children', unpublished doctoral dissertation, Edinburgh University.

Kamin, L.J. (1974) *The Science and Politics of IQ*, Harmondsworth: Penguin.

Kohlberg, L. (1969) *Stages in the Development of Moral Thought and Action*, New York: Holt.

Kohn, M.L. (1969) *Class and Conformity: A Study in Values*, Homewood, IL: Dorsey.

Latane, B. and Darley, J.M. (1968) 'Group inhibitions of bystander intervention in emergencies', *Journal of Personal and Social Psychology* 10: 215–21.

MacRae, A.W. (1994) 'Common misconceptions about statistics', ed. D. Hatcher, Proceedings of the ATP Conference, Birmingham University, July, pp. 1–12.

Marsh, P., Rosser, E. and Harre, R. (1978) *The Rules of Disorder*, London and New York: Routledge.

Michaels, J.W., Blommel, J.M., Broccato, R.M., Linkous, R.A. and Rowe, J.S. (1982) 'Social facilitation and inhibition in a natural setting', *Replications in Social Psychology* 2: 21–4.

Milgram, S. (1963) 'Behavioural study of obedience', *Journal of Abnormal and Social Psychology* 67: 371–8.

Monk, A. (1991) *Exploring Statistics with Minitab*, Chichester: John Wiley.

Murstein, B.I. (1972) 'Physical attractiveness and marital choice', *Journal of Personal and Social Psychology* 22: 8–12.

Orne, M.T. (1962) 'On the social psychology of the psychological experiment', *American Psychologist* 17 (11): 776–83.

—— (1966) 'Hypnosis, motivation and compliance', *American Journal of Psychiatry* 122: 721–6.

Peterson, L.R. and Peterson, M.J. (1959) 'Short-term retention of individual items', *Journal of Experimental Psychology* 58: 193–8.

Piaget, J. (1951) *Play, Dreams and Imitation in Childhood*, trans. C. Gattegno and F.M. Hodgson, New York: Norton, 1962.

Piliavin, I.M., Rodin, J. and Piliavin, J.A. (1969) 'Good Samaritism: An underground phenomena?', *Journal of Personal and Social Psychology* 13: 289–99.

Potter, J. and Wetherall, M. (1987) *Discourse and Social Analysis*, London: Sage.

Powell, F.C. (1976) *Cambridge Mathematical and Statistical Tables*, Cambridge: Cambridge University Press.

Robertson, J. and Robertson, J. (1971) 'Young children in brief separation: A fresh look', *Psychoanalytic Study of the Child* 26: 264–315.

Rosenhan, D.L. (1973) 'On being sane in insane places', *Science* 179: 250–8.

Rosenthal, R. (1966) *Experimenter Effects in Behavioural Research*, New York: Appleton-Century-Croft.

Schaffer, H.R. and Emerson, P.E. (1964) *The Development of Social Attachments in Infancy*, Monographs of the Society for Research in Child Development 29 (3), serial no. 94.

Shields, J. (1962) *Monozygotic Twins Brought Up Apart and Brought Up Together*, Oxford: Oxford University Press.

Siegel, S. (1956) *Non-parametric Statistics for the Behavioural Sciences*, New York: McGraw-Hill.

Silverman, I. (1977) 'Why social psychology fails', *Canadian Psychological Review* 18: 353–8.

Skeels, H.M. (1966) *Adult Status of Children with Contrasting Early Life Experiences*, Monograph of the Society for Research in Child Development 31 (3).

Smith, J.A. (1995) 'Qualitative methods, identity and transition to motherhood', *The Psychologist* 8 (3): 122–6.

Valentine, E.R. (1982) *Conceptual Issues in Psychology*, London and New York: Routledge.

Williams, T.M. (ed.) (1986) *The Impact of Television*, New York: Academic Press.

Zhar, J.H. (1972) 'Significance testing of the Spearman rank correlation coefficient', *Journal of the American Statistical Association* 67: 578–80.

Zimbardo, P.G., Banks, W.G., Craig, H. and Jaffe, D. (1973) 'A Pirandellian prison: The mind is a formidable jailor', *New York Times Mag.*, April 8th, 38–60.

Answers to exercises

Exercise 1
1 Quantitative; 2 Qualitative; 3 Qualitative; 4 Quantitative

Exercise 2
Reasons why observations made in everyday life might be flawed could include the fact that:

- they are based on a limited number of people;
- the event may only have been observed once;
- the observations have probably been made in one particular setting and on one subcultural group;
- the observation may be hearsay (you did not see the event yourself but were told about it);
- the observer may be biased;
- the observation will not have been carefully planned.

Exercise 3o
Alternative hypothesis The quality of the broth is better when it is made by a few cooks than when it is made by a lot of cooks.
Null hypothesis There is no difference in the quality of the broth made by a few cooks or by a lot of cooks.

(Variations on the above which mention both the broth and the number of cooks involved are acceptable too.)

Exercise 4

1   There could be several correct ways to phrase each hypothesis but they should be 'operationalised' – that is they should mention the variables being studied. If you are in doubt about your answers check with your lecturer.

(a)   *Directional hypothesis*: Students who eat a lot of fish obtain significantly higher IQ scores than students who never eat fish.
Non-directional hypothesis: There is a difference between the IQ scores of students who eat a lot of fish and those who never eat fish. (NB: the word 'significant' could be included.)
Null hypothesis: There is no difference in the IQ scores of students who eat a lot of fish and those who never eat fish.

(b)   *Directional hypothesis*: Babies spend longer looking at human faces than at simple shapes.
Non-directional hypothesis: There is a difference between the time babies spend looking at simple shapes and at human faces.
Null hypothesis: There is no difference in the amount of time babies spend looking at simple shapes or human faces.

(c)   *Directional hypothesis*: Tomato plants which are grown in the ground produce more tomatoes than those grown in 'grow bags'.
Non-directional hypothesis: There is a difference in the number of tomatoes produced by tomato plants grown in the ground and those grown in 'grow bags'.
Null hypothesis: There is no difference in the number of tomatoes produced by tomato plants grown in the ground or in 'grow bags'.

(d)   *Directional hypothesis*: There is a significant positive correlation between IQ at the age of eleven and IQ at the age of sixteen.
Non-directional hypothesis: There is a significant correlation between IQ at the age of eleven and IQ at the age of sixteen. (NB: the word 'significant' could be omitted.)
Null hypothesis: There is no correlation between IQ at the age of eleven and IQ at the age of sixteen.

(e)   *Directional hypothesis*: The higher the fares for the bus journey the fewer number of passengers use the bus service, or There is a negative correlation between the fares for the bus journey and the number of passengers using the bus service.
Non-directional hypothesis: There is a correlation between the fares for the bus journey and the number of passengers using the bus service.
Null hypothesis: There is no correlation between the fares for the bus journey and the number of passengers using the bus service.

2   (a) Directional
     (b) Directional
     (c) Directional
     (d) Non-Directional
     (e) Non-Directional

Exercise 5

1   IV = being kept awake or normal sleep; DV = memory of the word list.
2   IV = having run a mile or driven a car for a mile; DV = reaction time.
3   IV = size of bug; DV = bugs chosen to be eaten.
4   IV = whether the participant is told the person is of the same or different
     ethnic group; DV = characteristics selected.
5   IV = size of group; DV = number of cereal packets packed in thirty
     minutes.

Exercise 6

Answers will depend on the experiments selected. You should discuss your
answers with other students in a small group or as a class exercise.

Exercise 7

1   Quasi-experiment (random allocation of participants to groups is not
     possible)
2   Natural experiment (the IV is not manipulated by the researchers)
3   Natural experiment
4   Quasi-experiment

Exercise 8

1   Discuss your answers in a small group or in class
2   (a) Naturalistic observation
     (b) Naturalistic observation
     (c) Experiment using the observational technique
     (d) Controlled observation
     (e) Experiment using the observational technique

Exercise 9

Not easy! There are a range of acceptable answers to this exercise. The important point is that you need to define 'aggression' and think of a way in which
your definition can be operationalised into observable behaviour.

For example, Baron (1977) defines aggression as 'any form of behaviour
that is directed towards the goal of harming or injuring another living thing
who is motivated to avoid such treatment'.

1   If you based your study on this definition you would not include injury
     to inanimate objects and might not include 'play fighting'. (In this latter
     case is the person being hit 'motivated to avoid such treatment'?) You
     might include hitting, pushing, etc. that is directed towards someone

trying to avoid it. You might also not include verbal aggression. Does this fit into the definition above?

2   This is a bit easier. You might include biting, pouncing, scratching, etc. that is aimed at another creature trying to escape.

Exercise 10

1   Your answers might include:

Having several observers and checking inter-judge reliability; ensuring the state of the pitch was similar; the importance of the game to the players; whether a scout from a premier league club was watching; the weather; and so on. Any sensible answers are acceptable.

2   Definitions in the glossary.

Exercise 11

1   *Time interval sampling*: a child is observed for several periods of two minutes each.

Event sampling: each time a certain action is observed it is noted.

Time point sampling: a child is observed every two minutes (at 2 mins, 4 mins, 6 mins, etc.) and any aggressive behaviour is noted.

2   Inter-judge reliability could be a problem because different judges might disagree as to whether a certain behaviour was aggression or not. This can be checked by comparing the two judges' ratings and making sure that there is a close correlation between them.

3   Possible qualitative data could concern interpretations of children's intentions by observers, interviews with children about their feelings during the period observed, and so on.

Exercise 12

This exercise could be done in a small group or as a class exercise. You should be able to work out the answers from the text.

Exercise 13

1   The answers are in the text.

2   This exercise can be done in a small group or as a class exercise. The answers obviously depend on the type of interview selected in the first part of the question.

Exercise 14

1   Positive
2   Negative
3   Negative
4   Negative
5   Positive

3   It *could* be the case that television teaches safe driving habits, but it could also be true that people who watch a lot of TV spend less time driving and this is the reason for the lower number of accidents; that people with young children watch more TV and that the presence of children in the car makes them careful drivers; and so on. It is correlational evidence and thus cause-and-effect relationships cannot be assumed.

The answers are not necessarily clear-cut, as the nature of quantitative and qualitative methods varies a great deal from study to study. Discuss possible answers in a small group or in class.

1   Repeated measures
2   Independent groups
3   Repeated measures
4   Matched pairs
5   Independent groups
6   Independent groups

Check your answers with the advantages and disadvantages given in the text. Possible answers include:

1   The participants are given anagrams to solve when they are hungry and when they have just eaten. No problems with differences in the ability of participants to solve anagrams as they all take part in each condition, but they might guess what the study is about and so results are affected by demand characteristics. You would have to devise two lists of anagrams of equal difficulty as they couldn't do the same list twice.
2   Participants' anagram-solving ability has been controlled, but the earlier testing necessary would make the study rather complicated. You only need one list of anagrams.
3   Here Group A might solve the anagrams with no practice, Group B after one practice session and Group C after two practice sessions. As each group is only solving one set of anagrams there should be fewer problems related to demand characteristics, and they can all use the same set of anagrams. However, you might end up with all the good anagram-solvers in one condition and all the bad ones in another.

1   You don't want to spend twenty years conducting a study and *then* find a flaw!
2   The differences that you find between the groups may be due to a variable other than age.

3   Different age groups may have different life experiences. People born at the same time and in the same place will have experienced similar cultural and historic influences and may share similar thoughts and behaviours due to these influences.

4   Answers in the text.

Exercise 20

1   All male and female readers.
2   All cats.
3   All cat owners.
4   Agoraphobics who receive cognitive therapy.
5   All one-year-old infants.

Exercise 21

Answers in the text.

Exercise 22

1   See text.
2   It would be a biased sample. Volunteer sample.
3   See text.
4   *Random sample*: give each student at the college a number and then select fifty using random number tables.

   Stratified sample: work out the percentages of male/female students, different age groups, different subjects studied, and so on. Select students by random sampling so each variable is represented in the sample in the same proportion as it is represented in the population as a whole. For example, if 6 per cent of the population is women over forty years old then you must identify these women and select three using random sampling.

   Quota sample: As above – but you can select the sample using opportunity sampling.

   Opportunity sample: Ask the first fifty students you meet that you feel brave enough to ask to take part.

Exercise 23

Possible answers include:

1   Women might not wish to discuss some aspects of pregnancy with a man.
2   The children might see they are being watched and so behave differently to usual.
3   Men might want to impress her and so try particularly hard.
4   Do I really need to tell you the answer?

1   The participants must not know if they have been drinking *Memorade* or a placebo.
2   The people with the sprains don't know whether they are being massaged with improved *Spraineze* or original formula *Spraineze* – and neither do the people judging how quickly they recover.

1   Get someone else to mark the essay and see if the two marks agree. Get your friend to submit the same essay and see if it gets the same mark.
2   A finding which is replicated is reliable.
3   You could give it to the same group on two occasions and see if they give similar answers each time (test/re-test reliability), or you could compare the answers on the odd and even questions (split-half reliability).

1   No. There might be several reasons it wants to go out at that time. For example perhaps it often has a walk about then. Just because a finding is reliable does not mean it is a valid measure.
2   Correlate the two sets of results.
3   It could measure how anxious someone is at a particular moment and thus be valid – but, if that person's anxiety varies from situation to situation, the results could vary and thus not be reliable.
4   An IQ test could give consistent results, but not actually be measuring someone's IQ (e.g. it could be measuring language skills).

1   One group drink *Coca Cola* and then *Pepsi*, while the others drink *Pepsi* then *Coca Cola*.
2   Some mark Essay A then Essay B; others mark Essay B then Essay A.
3   Some are shown the triangle then the circle; others are shown the circle then the triangle.

1   See text and glossary.
2   Answers could include:

(a)   Eyesight, interest in cars or dogs, ownership of a collie, having recently been involved in a car crash, and so on.
        The best control is probably random allocation of the participants.

(b)   Your participants are car mechanics.
        Pick your participants by random sampling.

(c)   The order of presentation should be counterbalanced: some see Clip A then Clip B; others see Clip B then Clip A.

Exercise 29

1   Deception, no informed consent, stress. Have parents or those *in loco parentis* been asked for consent? Can the eleven- and twelve-year-olds withdraw or ask for their results not to be used? Is there any debriefing?

2   Deception, no informed consent, stress. (Though it might do potential psychological researchers good to experience what it feels like to be on the receiving end!)

3   No informed consent, possible stress, difficult to withdraw from the study. Is there any debriefing?

Exercise 30

Possible answers include:

Figure 9.17   The graph is meaningless as it has participants along the bottom axis. There is no title.

Table of results   What do the numbers stand for? Of what are they the results? There is no measure of the dispersion of scores.

Histogram to show favourite animals   This is not a histogram. The vertical axis is not labelled. Why are the categories shown at the top? Whose favourite animals are represented here?

Exercise 31

Check your answers are correct with someone else.

Exercise 32

Check your answers are correct with the text or with your teacher.

Exercise 33a

1   See text.

2   (a)   Mean = 8; median = 6; mode = 6
       (b)   Mean = 6.09; median = 6; mode = 7
       (c)   Mean = 8.92; median = 9.5; mode = 12

Exercise 33b

1   (a)   Positive skew
       (b)   Roughly normal distribution
       (c)   Negative skew

2   (a)   Bimodal distribution
       (b)   Almost a normal distribution

Exercise 34

1   47.72 per cent

2   2.28 per cent

3   68.26 per cent

4   65 – Low (in the bottom 2.28 per cent); 110 – Fairly high (in the top 50 per cent); 120 – High (in the top 15.87 per cent); 144 – Very high (in the top 2.28 per cent)

1   15.87 per cent
2   13.59 per cent
3   2.28 per cent
4   68.26 per cent

1(a)

Group A	Range = 73 − 35 = 38
Group B	Range = 75 − 30 = 45

(b)   The range is affected by extreme scores. The two ranges above are only crude representations of the spread of scores, which do not reflect the differences in the distribution of the two sets of scores.
2   See text or glossary.
3   Above 48 = 2.28 per cent; below 36 = 15.87 per cent; between 32 and 40 = 47.72 per cent
4(b) Over 30 = 15.87 per cent; between 30 and 35 = 13.59 per cent; under 25 = 50 per cent

1(a) Ratio   (also   interval);   (b) Nominal;   (c) Interval;   (d) Ordinal; (e) Nominal; (f) Ordinal.
2   Possible answers are:

(a)   Who passed or failed their driving test is recorded.
(b)   Experts rate driving skills on a scale of 1 to 10.
(c)   The time taken to drive round an obstacle course is measured.

1   Nominal, independent data – therefore chi-square would be appropriate.
2   Ordinal data, repeated measures design – therefore Wilcoxon matched pairs signed ranks test would be appropriate.
3   Ordinal data, independent measures design – therefore Mann–Whitney test would be appropriate.
4   Ordinal data, correlational design – therefore Spearman's rho would be appropriate.
5   Ordinal data, correlational design – therefore Spearman's rho would be appropriate. (If the tests used were fully standardised some statisticians would argue that the data was interval and thus Pearson's product moment should be used.)
6   Digit span is not true interval data as it gets harder to remember numbers as the number of digits increases. Thus it is common to regard this as ordinal data. As there is an independent groups design, the Mann–Whitney test would be used. (Some people *might*

argue that digit span is sufficiently close to interval data that the *t*-test for independent samples could be used – given that this is a robust test.)

Exercise 39

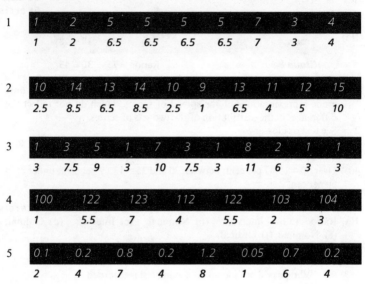

1	1	2	5	5	5	5	7	3	4
	1	2	6.5	6.5	6.5	6.5	7	3	4
2	10	14	13	14	10	9	13	11	12	15
	2.5	8.5	6.5	8.5	2.5	1	6.5	4	5	10
3	1	3	5	1	7	3	1	8	2	1	1
	3	7.5	9	3	10	7.5	3	11	6	3	3
4	100	122	123	112	122	103	104
	1	5.5	7	4	5.5	2	3
5	0.1	0.2	0.8	0.2	1.2	0.05	0.7	0.2
	2	4	7	4	8	1	6	4

Exercise 40

$0.01 = 1$ per cent or $\frac{1}{1000}$; $0.025 = 2.5$ per cent or $\frac{1}{100}$; $0.20 = 20$ per cent or $\frac{1}{200}$; $0.001 = 0.1$ per cent or $\frac{1}{5}$; $0.005 = 0.5$ per cent or $\frac{1}{40}$

Exercise 41

1	0.10	0.05	0.02	0.01	0.002	0.001

2   0.10 is the most lenient
3   0.001 is the most stringent

Exercise 42
1   The answers are in the text. This exercise would be best done in a small group or as a class exercise.
2   Possible answers include categorising answers and selecting examples.

Exercise 43

(a) Data could be presented in a table or perhaps a bar chart. Chi-square might be used.
(b) This would produce quantitative data which could be analysed using descriptive and/or inferential statistics.
(c) As above, but the use of parametric statistics might be possible.
(d) Categorise answers; give examples; etc.

Index

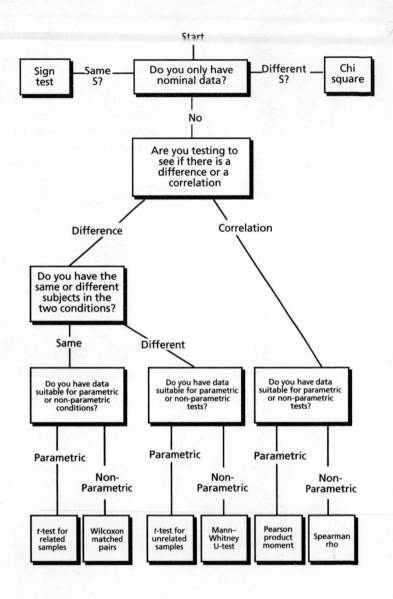